DOCTORS AND THE BMA

A Case Study in Collective Action

Doctors and the BMA

A Case Study in Collective Action

PHILIP R. JONES

University of Bath

Gower

Published by
Gower Publishing Company Limited,
Westmead, Farnborough, Hants, England

British Library Cataloguing in Publication Data

Jones, Philip R.
Doctors and the BMA.
1. British Medical Association
2. Social choice - Case studies
I. Title
331. 88'1161'0941   R35.B83

ISBN 0-566-00338-4

Printed in Great Britain by Biddles Ltd, Guildford, Surrey

Contents

Acknowledgements

In pursuing this research I have benefited from many
sources. My greatest debt is owed to Mr John Bonner of
the Department of Economics at Leicester University. His
help and guidance has contributed significantly to whatever
merit this work possesses. I have also profited from the
help of Professor Dennis Lees of Nottingham University who
has constructively commented on the work. My thanks go
also to Mr S.W.F. Holloway for his insights to the history
of the medical profession and to Sir Stanley Dennison who
kindly drew on his experiences as a member of the Review
Body on Doctors and Dentists Remuneration. The staff of
the Economics Departments of Hull University and Bath
University have also offered encouragement. Errors that
remain, of course, exist in spite of the good advice offered.

The British Medical Association assisted me with the
distribution of a questionnaire survey to doctors, and also
put their library at my disposal. Personnel of the General
Practitioners Association, Junior Hospital Doctors
Association, Hospital Consultants Specialist Association
and General Medical Council also kindly obliged me with
information.

1 Introduction

1.1 COLLECTIVE ACTION AND COLLECTIVE AWARENESS

Even the most cursory review of literature on the question
of collective behaviour reflects the wide range of
disciplines from which contributions have been made. Authors
associated with areas of study such as sociology, psychology,
politics, the study of industrial relations and economics
have looked at the question of why individuals might engage
in collective activity. Nevertheless within this diverse
literature it is possible to note at least two main lines of
approach to the question. The first of these is one which
focuses attention on the environment of individuals. It is
held that factors in the environment of individuals will
determine whether or not they are likely to choose to join
associations. Changes in the environment will influence
demand for membership of associations. Individuals' desires
or wants are taken to be related to the circumstances in
which they live. As such one asks the question what factors
determine the demand for an association.

Just such a question has been asked with respect to many
groups of individuals. Professor David Lockwood (1966) for
example, in seeking to explain membership of clerical unions,
looked to changes in the work environment of clerks. He
noted that membership had increased at a time when the
individual relationship clerks had entertained with their
work and with their employers had been transformed. It had
been transformed into a bureaucratic environment of
standardised functions with common rules and regulations and
with no personal contact with employers. As such it was
argued that clerks now recognised common interests with
other clerks. They recognised common interests in terms of
a common stipulated wage for particular functions, or in
terms of common working conditions to perform duties.
Hence he claims that 'bureaucratisation' represented a set of
conditions extremely favourable to the growth of collective
action among clerical workers. He argues that concerted
action "ultimately depends on the awareness of individuals
that they have interests in common; and therefore that they
belong together." (1)

The existence of collective interests for a group of
individuals is then an important feature in explaining
collective action, and in similar vein other writers looking
to other groups have concentrated on isolating in the
environment the factor which has created collective interests.
Work environment has proved an important influence on the
existence of collective awareness and hence on the
propensity of individuals to join associations. For example,
the survey for the Royal Commission on Trade Unions and
Employers Associations in 1967 found 63 per cent of trade
unionists in their sample worked in establishments with a

1

100 or more workers, and 64 per cent of the non-unionists were working in establishments with less than 100 workers. (2)   Routh (1962) not only notes aspects of an individual's work environment, e.g. the size of the establishment where work is conducted, the degree of skill involved in the work, but also the nature of the occupation of parents, and the area of residence. Indeed, the influence of social background on membership of trade unions and voluntary associations is a variable which has been investigated by many authors. (3)   The rationale, of course, is based on the argument that certain backgrounds create a collective awareness, i.e. an awareness on the part of the individual that he has common interests with other members of a particular group. (4)

Some studies specifically seek the stimulus of this collective awareness in the existence of a collective threat. Trueman (1951) for example, explains the formation of associations as the reaction of some individuals to a political or economic threat which they feel collectively. Davis (1941) has similarly suggested that the relationship between rising prices and the growth of unions is based on the reaction by groups of individuals to an attack on their real incomes. (5)   Seidman, London and Karsh (1951) note the importance in stimulating union membership of a threat or unfair treatment from supervisors.

However, the environment can be examined not only in terms of whether or not it influences the demand for membership of associations, but also whether or not it is conducive to the supply of associations. F. Castles (1967) for example, stresses the importance of the political climate to the emergence of associations. Within totalitarian regimes there are barriers to their formation. In under developed countries, where illiteracy is high, communications poor, and hence political awareness dormant, the development of associations is inevitably restricted. In similar terms K. Prandy (1965) and G.S. Bain (1970) have noted the attitudes of employers to membership in trade unions. For example, white collar workers, fearing that promotion will be blocked by membership may not pursue collective aims by joining associations. Furthermore, the likelihood that membership of an association grows must be heavily dependent on the way in which the association's services are sold. (6) The appearance of good leadership and sound constitution in associations may be vital in persuading individuals that membership will lead to the attainment of collective aims and interests.

A recent study by G.S. Bain and F. Elsheikh (1979) reflects the development of this approach. Not only do they note many of the above variables, they also seek to indicate their relative importance. They look, for example, to the influence of the business cycle. It is argued that when there is unemployment union members may feel that via their contribution to the union they have less chance of gaining

2

their common goal and to this extent may be less prepared
to join. Reference is made also to the size of
establishment, in so far as employees in larger
establishments are more likely to be treated not as
individuals, but as members of the group to which they
belong. In considering the environment in which unions
grow attention is drawn to the market in which unions find
themselves. Oligopolistic or monopolistic employers, for
example, may have greater financial resources to resist
initial union organisation. In seeking to estimate the
effect of wages, unemployment, age, sex, part time
employment and market structure on union membership,
multiple regression models for twenty two industries (or,
when the wages variable was used, for twenty one industries)
for 1951, 1961 and 1971 can be applied to indicate the
significance of such variables. However, such a study
appears a direct extension of the theme to which reference
has been made. It is in keeping with the view that the
general environment in which individuals find themselves
makes them aware of collective interests and may also prove
conducive to the pursuit of these common goals.

1.2 COLLECTIVE ACTION AND COLLECTIVE GOODS

The second form of analysis which can be identified in the
literature on collective behaviour is one which moves
emphasis from the environment of the individual to the goal
which the individual hopes to attain. Rather than searching
for those forces in society which transmit a desire or
awareness on the part of the individual that he may benefit
from the attainment of a collective goal, it focuses
attention on the nature of such a goal. This form of
approach was pioneered by M. Olson Jr. (7) It was his
observation that "the achievement of any common goal or the
satisfaction of any common interest means that a public or
collective good has been provided for that group." (8) He
defined a collective or public good completely in terms of
the "non-exclusion principle." (9) That is to say that
should the good be provided to any one individual, then
there was no means by which its consumption could be
restricted to other individuals. Thus, for example, a group
of workers may have a common interest in attaining a higher
wage, but, once attained, that wage rate might be received
by anyone taking the job. Similarly a group of individuals
might have an interest in lobbying for favourable
legislation, but when achieved all are able to enjoy the
benefit of the legislation. The fact that a goal or purpose
is common to a group means that no one in the group is
excluded from the benefit or satisfaction brought about by
its attainment.

This observation of Olson has quite important implications.
The question of whether or not an individual will choose to
pursue common interests by subscribing to an association is
exactly the same as the question of whether or not an
individual will voluntarily contribute to the provision of a

collective good. Given the definition of the good and given assumptions concerning the nature of individuals, certain predictions can be made with respect to this question. Assume for example it is possible to identify a group of individuals who wish to provide a collective good. Each individual is initially defined in terms of a selfish or pure economic man, i.e. he is neither malevolent nor benevolent and is concerned only with his own independent utility function. It may be accepted also that each wishes to maximize his utility and that he acts rationally. (10) If an association is formed, it is assumed that this is merely a vehicle for the provision of the collective good, i.e. the analysis is individualistic and recognises no other aims than those of the individuals involved. Each individual will only subscribe to the association, and hence contribute to the provision of the collective good, if the increment in utility derived from such action is greater than the opportunity cost involved. However, he is aware that if the good is provided he will enjoy that increment of utility whether or not he has undertaken the opportunity cost. There is therefore an element of doubt as to whether or not he will make the contribution and join the association. His strategy may instead be to allow others to cover the costs incurred by the provision of the collective goal, and to enjoy the good so produced without any personal sacrifice. As such the individual would hope to "free ride".

This argument is not independent of the question of the size of the group. If the group is small, it has been argued that, other things being equal, the individual can expect a more "significant proportion of the total benefit from the collective good." (11) In this case the increment in utility he enjoys from this good may more than cover the total cost of providing the good. Hence, rather than not see the good provided at all, the individual would cover these costs himself, or if possible cover them by some agreement with individuals in a similar situation. There is then the likelihood that the good may be provided, and that this may be as a result of the association of individuals. There are other arguments that support the proposition that the voluntary provision of collective goods is more likely when the group is small. For example, it may be suggested here, and later proved more rigorously, that, if an individual feels that his share of the costs involved is more significant in a smaller group, then he may more readily participate. Furthermore, the case that small groups are more effective in providing collective goods may be supported by the argument that bargaining costs between individuals would be lower in smaller groups. It is not argued that small groups necessarily provide themselves with collective goods in an optimal fashion, but merely that they will tend to provide some quantity of the good. On the other hand, the large group, where no one individual would cover the total costs of provision of the good, and where each individual feels that his contribution to the costs is of no significance, will remain latent. The irony of such

4

an outcome is that, even in the large group situation it can be shown that the total benefit to be accrued by the individuals concerned may outweigh the total costs involved, and still the large group remains immobilised in the pursuit of its collective aim.

This analysis then introduces a dichotomy. On the one hand it is proposed that collective behaviour is a response to common aims, and on the other it is argued that in large groups common aims will not induce collective action from large groups. One approach throws weight on those factors which stimulate demand for collective goods and on an environment which supports organisation. The other emphasises the characteristics of the common goal and the size of the group, and asserts boldly that awareness of collective interests will not explain collective action because of the problems inherent in revealing demand for such collective goods. Something of the flavour of this dichotomy is to be found in alternative views of society. There are those who would stress the argument that societies emerge because individuals share a consensus of opinion, a similarity in views and objectives. There are those who would stress the reverse, i.e. that social intercourse between individuals is dependent rather on the differences between individuals; that individuals have different skills and different resources, such that trading between all can be to their mutual advantage. In this sense individuals act collectively not so much as a reflection of a desire to attain common ends, but as a result of the fact that each may individually benefit by dealing with others.

As well as introducing this dichotomy the collective choice literature leads to many more questions concerning the provision of common goals. In the first instance the theory that in certain circumstances individuals will not voluntarily contribute to the pursuit of common goals must be reconciled with the observation that voluntary associations exist. Secondly, if there are situations in which subscription is voluntarily undertaken, will the goal be achieved efficiently, or if not, in what way will the outcome deviate from the efficient solution? Implicit in these questions are the basic problems of providing mechanisms to lead individuals to reveal their preferences for collective goods.

1.3   THE BRITISH MEDICAL ASSOCIATION: A CASE STUDY

It is in the light of the predictions that are generated from collective choice theory that the British Medical Association was selected as a case study. Empirical testing of these predictions is difficult for reasons that become clear in this study. Such evidence as there is tends to be in the form of casual observations of the behaviour of a number of pressure groups or associations. (12)   Close scrutiny of one association may therefore prove beneficial. The experience of the BMA stands as the experiment in collective action which is to be placed under the microscope. While not arguing that the evidence analysed will in itself prove a completely satisfactory test for the above theoretical discussion, it is hoped that it will yield some important insights. The analysis may later be compared with that of other associations to add weight to such results. Case studies can provocatively question widely held opinions. Within the general field of collective choice theory Ronald Coase's (1974) examination of the provision of lighthouse services is an extremely important example. Theoretical predictions of the impossibility of providing such services except via general tax funding have been called into question as a result of analysis of the history of lighthouse provision. (13)

The British Medical Association was chosen as a suitable case study for at least three reasons. Firstly, membership to the BMA is deemed voluntary and, at least at the outset, there is every reason to believe that the decision to join is left with the individual doctor. That is to say that doctors can legally remain in practice without joining the BMA. There is then a recognisable group of individuals, i.e. those qualified to practice medicine, who via an Association, the BMA, voluntarily contribute to the pursuit of collective goods.

A second advantage of looking to the BMA is that within their activities they pursue a wide range of objectives typical of pressure groups and trade unions. They negotiate on the working conditions and remuneration of doctors, and monitor such agreements. They attempt to influence government policy on questions of the provision of medical care and health. They also provide an array of services, such as individual advice and social meetings.

Thirdly, and not at all of least importance, the observation that the Association appears successful in terms of mobilizing medical practitioners. In absolute terms its membership has stood as high as 76,673 members, while in relative terms Association membership has represented some 80 per cent of the medical profession. (14) This feat is no mean achievement. Compare briefly the position of the BMA at its origins with that of the early 1970's.

(a)   The British Medical Association: Early days.

At Worcester Infirmary in 1832 Dr Charles Hastings proposed the inauguration of a new medical association to a small group of some fifty medical gentlemen. The purpose of such a venture was quite clearly to provide a stimulus to research into all aspects of medicine and also a vehicle for the dissemination of new information. Hope was expressed that this association might serve to maintain the honour of the profession in the provinces of England and Wales, and the doctors of Worcester chose to call their association, the Provincial Medical and Surgical Association.

6

There was little that was new in the establishment of a
medical society in the provinces. Such medical research and
education clubs may be traced to the last third of the
eighteenth century. (15)   In 1770 the doctors of Warrington
had established just such a society, and they had been
emulated in 1774 by the medical men of Colchester. In 1794
a similar society was founded in Plymouth and again in 1800
in Leicester. By 1822 Halifax and District followed suit
as did St Helens in 1826 and Nottingham in 1828. According
to J.L. Thornton (1949) the Provincial Medical and Surgical
Association in 1832 took its place alongside another forty
medical societies in Britain.

In the tradition of many other medical societies the PMSA
published an annual volume of transactions; the first
appearing in 1833. However, on October 3, 1840, a new
weekly publication, The Provincial Medical and Surgical
Journal appeared. This journal took upon itself the
function of providing a means of communication of medical
ideas as well as distributing news of medical societies, and
of course in particular, news of the PMSA. Yet even at this
time there were seven medical periodicals published in Great
Britain, of which three appeared quarterly, one fortnightly,
and three weekly. The PMSA found significant problems in
establishing itself as a competitor. Between 1847 and 1855,
for reasons of economy, it became a fortnightly journal.
By 1855, the Medical Times and Gazette published a leading
article on the decay of the PMSJ and recommended its
discontinuance. (16)

Indeed, reports suggest that the future of the PMSA was
very much in the balance during these early years. In 1836,
for example, The Lancet, referred to the "total failure" of
the PMSA. (17)   Whilst criticism of the young Association
and its Journal may in part be due to aggressive competition
from contemporaries, there is, nevertheless, evidence to
collaborate some of the views expressed. In 1882
Dr William Strange, for example, recalled to members of the
Association that in the early years: "The meetings were
small; and the communications with signal exceptions were
only second rate; whilst the journal which contained them
was as frequently uncut and unread as not." (18)

It appeared that two important ventures of the Association
had soon met with failure. By 1859 only 174 subscribers
could be found to the Medical Benevolent Fund of the
society; a fact that was strongly criticised by the
committee of the PMSA. (19)   Yet as early as 1836 the hopes
of providing library facilities were dashed when a committee
reported the insurmountable difficulties involved, and
recommended that this plan be shelved.   (20)

The growth of membership of the PMSA can at best be
described as slow. By 1853, that is after twenty one years,
it still had considerably less than two thousand members.(21)
The Medical Directory for that year showed that there were
at least 11,808 qualified doctors practising throughout the

7

country. (22)   In fact, membership of the PMSA had begun
to fall slightly in 1852. (23)   By 1853 there was a
movement to broaden the basis of the society. Initially
the Association had been designed primarily for provincial
doctors. In London the medical world had been dominated by
the two Royal Colleges, i.e. the Royal College of Physicians
and the Royal College of Surgeons. However in 1853 doctors
in the metropolis were formally invited to join the
Association. By 1855, when membership was still only 2,125
and again falling, (24) the Association, not without some
remorse on the part of older members, adopted the name of
the British Medical Association. The headquarters of the
Association moved from Worcester to London, and on January 3,
1857, the Journal of the Association adopted the title of
the British Medical Journal.

(b)   The British Medical Association: Today

The BMA is today a body of some 63,000 medical gentlemen,(25)
and as such it is said to represent the second largest
medical association in the world. (26)   While absolute
membership is large, the density of membership is also high.
In order to indicate the importance of the BMA in national
medical political life two measures of density appear useful.
First, in terms of the percentage membership of doctors in
the United Kingdom the BMA has had a membership density of
77 per cent in 1950,(27) and in 1973 this figure remained
as high as 68 per cent.(28)   Secondly, in terms of the
percentage of the working profession in the United Kingdom
the BMA recorded 85 per cent in 1950,(29) and in 1973 was
still able to boast an impressive 70 per cent.(30)

   Either in terms of absolute membership or membership
density the BMA is today a formidable body. Similarly its
success has been matched by that of the BMJ. In 1979 for
example this journal's circulation was 86,607.(31)   The
BMJ is no longer the only journal published by the BMA. It
has been joined by many specialist journals as well as a
widely popular Family Doctor Booklet series.

   The BMA receives over £1.6 million in membership
subscriptions and this together with income from rents,
investments, and surpluses on publications provides a total
of over £2.8 million. (32)   In 1979 proposals were made
to raise the standard rate of subscription from £50 to £70.
However, the costs of its secretariat have obviously risen
and particularly so during this century. In 1904 there
were only two full time officials in the BMA, by 1960 there
were twenty three and today the salary bill of the BMA is
£1.8 million per annum. (33)   Within the UK thirty five
branches extend outwards from its headquarters; though
branches are found in all corners of the world. The BMA
calendar testifies to the numerous specialist committees
which deal with everything from the ethical problems of the
profession to the narrow problems of small medical

specialities. While outside the BMA representatives are to be found on an inordinate number of committees, e.g. quite recently they have taken seats on the Standing Committee of Doctors of the Common Market. (34)

The BMA still takes its place alongside many other medical societies, but today "the BMA is by far the largest and most powerful of the doctors' organisations." (35) The medical world is inundated by an ubiquitous distribution of associations which for convenience may be classified within three groups. Firstly, the prestigious Royal Colleges are still in evidence. Their main function is that of qualifying bodies and supervisors of post-graduate medical education. Their political voice is not dismissed, though it is more quietly and more infrequently exercised. Indeed when it is exercised it is generally with regard to the interests of the consultant hierarchy of the profession. Beneath the grandeur of the Royal Colleges one finds a body of associations such as the British Post-Graduate Medical Federation, the Faculty of Opthalmologists, the Apothecaries Society, the Society of Medical Officers of Health, the Fellowship of Post-graduate Medicine. Such bodies neither attempt to exercise or indeed possess, a great deal of political influence. However, a third group which includes the BMA, does encompass those medical bodies who would wish to exert influence. This group includes such bodies as the Medical Practitioners Union (MPU), the Junior Hospital Doctors' Association (JHDA), the Hospital Consultants and Specialists Association (HCSA), the General Practitioners' Association (GPA), and the Socialist Medical Association (SMA). These infants, all of the twentieth century, have had far less influence than the BMA. It would be fair to assess their activity more often in terms of a "ginger group" to the BMA. None of these medico-political associations could boast one eleventh of the membership of the BMA (36) and as Forsythe insists, there is "no serious challenge to the British Medical Association as the representative of the British Doctor." (37)

The position of the BMA today, therefore stands in marked contrast to that of its humble origins. Perhaps the greatest tribute to its success, however, is inherent in the comment of Paul Vaughan: "in the minds of many people the British Medical Association has become synonymous with the medical profession in this country." (38)

1.4   OUTLINE OF THE STUDY

The growth of the BMA together with the influence it has exerted upon medical practice in the UK is a social phenomenon which merits research in itself. The position of prominence which the Association holds today is one which begs some investigation of its structure power and purpose. Its influence on decision taking in the National Health Service calls for examination, not least because of the

9

large sums of public expenditure involved. (39)   A history
of the BMA cannot ignore these aspects, but of course it is
primarily as a pre-requisite for a study of collective
choice theory that an interpretive account of the evolution
of the Association is provided in chapter two. As such the
account draws attention not only to the influence the
Association has had on the development of the National
Health Service, but also to the often neglected reciprocal
influence that this form of state intervention has had on
the professional Association. The history looks to the
growth of the Association and its acquisition of political
maturity and questions some popularly held views of the role
of the BMA and the State.

From a history of the Association the intention is to
highlight those factors that may have heightened the
collective awareness of doctors, and to say something of
their relative importance. We ask whether changes in the
demand for membership of the BMA can be related to changes
in doctors' work environment? What influence has the
development of professional consciousness had on membership?
To what extent might one explain membership growth in terms
of the social background of doctors? How important has the
intervention of the government in the medical market been
to the demand for membership of the BMA? These questions
are important, for even if they do not explain why
individuals contribute to common goals, they do indicate how
their demand for these goals may be shifted.

In chapter four a closer examination of the "free rider"
hypothesis is undertaken. This hypothesis leads to the
belief that demand will not be revealed in terms of
contribution or membership of the BMA. How is the
prediction affected by the numbers of individuals concerned?
How do assumptions about the degree to which the common goal
may be regarded as a pure public good affect the outcome?
Will the assumption about the common goal being indivisible
affect the prediction? How do assumptions about the
character of the individual affect the prediction e.g. if
the individual is deemed alturistic would the same
prediction be expected? Is it fair to consider the BMA
as an Association for which the predictions of the "free
rider" hypothesis may be expected and if so how can its
existence be reconciled with the hypothesis?

The difficulty of dealing with the last of these topics
will prove the substance of the following chapters five and
six. Here a much closer scrutiny is undertaken of the
assumption that indeed individuals freely choose to join
the Association. Though overtly not having closed shop
status the question arises as to whether or not informal
pressure can be brought to bear to ensure membership. Is
it the case that sanctions can and have been applied to non-
members? On the other hand the question is raised that
inducements can and have been offered to members in order
to promote membership. Are such inducements of importance
to members, such that membership can be explained in this

fashion? How acceptable is the logic of this argument that membership of associations pursuing collective goals can be explained in terms of the provision by the association of goods which might be excludable from non-members?

In the closing chapters of the book an attempt is made to introduce into the analysis the effect of leadership. The problem is tackled in terms of the possible effect that leadership might have on the perceptions of would be members. This is introduced with reference to the noted experience of the BMA and the dichotomy in analysis of collective behaviour. The introduction of leadership and the possibility that their goals may not be identical to those of the association membership raises a number of interesting implications for collective choice theory.

NOTES

1 D. Lockwood (1966) p.40
2 The results of the survey are quoted in J. Hughes (1973)
3 See for example: A.A. Blum, (1968), R.M. Blackburn (1967), Mark van de Vall, (1970), M. Hausknecht (1962)
4 "A worker's willingness to join a union varies directly with the degree to which association with and participation in the union would reinforce normal group attachments and interest." E. Wight Bakke, (1945) p.37
5 Note however, that the alternative causal link is possible, i.e. price rise as a consequence of union growth. Union growth may be taken as an index of union militancy putting pressure on wages and as a result on prices which manufacturers set. See G. Hines (1964)
6 It seems obvious that membership of an association will increase, at least in absolute terms, if it recruits from as wide a basis as possible. Nevertheless the importance of this has of late been stressed by John Hughes, (1973) p.8
   "One thing is surely clear. A structure of narrowly conceived industrial or occupational unionism may be a dead hand on union development. This form of unionism does not use its strength in organisational capacity in sector A to build or strengthen unionism in sector B... The main unions that have shown capacity for growth and development have been much more open in their recruitment approach......"
7 M. Olson Jr., The Logic of Collective Action, Harvard University Press, Massachusetts, 1965, (reprinted in 1971 with an added appendix).
8 M. Olson Jr. (1971) p.15
9 See R.A. Musgrave (1959)
10 Rational behaviour on the part of an individual may be summarily defined in terms of the following three conditions: (1) the individual evaluates alternatives on the basis of his preferences among them, (2) his preference ordering is consistent and transitive, and (3) he always chooses the preferred alternative. Such

a definition will later be looked at in more detail.
A discussion is to be found in A. Downs, (1957) p.6

11 M. Olson Jr (1971) p.34. See also, M. Olson Jr. and
     R. Zeckhauser, (1966)

12 M. Olson Jr. (1971) makes many observations of a number
     of associations, see in particular chapter 6. Wyn
     Grant and David Marsh (1977) undertake a case study of
     the CBI,the results of which are directly comparable
     with that of the BMA.

13 See also Alan Peacock (1979), Chapter 9

14 See, J. Blondel (1967) p.169 and BMJ (Supp) April 28
     1962, p.177

15 A. Batty Shaw, "The Oldest Medical Societies in Great
     Britain". Medical History, Vol.12, July 1968, and
     Sir Humphrey Rolleston, "Medical Friendships, Clubs and
     Societies", Annals of Medical History, Vol.11, May 1930

16 E.M. Little (1932) p.177

17 The Lancet, Nov.5 1836

18 The British Medical Journal, Vol.2, 1822, p.247

19 BMJ, August 6, 1859, p.636

20 The Provincial Medical and Surgical Journal, 1836,p.xxvi

21 Association Medical Journal 1845, Report of Council
     22 Sept., p.851 declares that the PMSA's membership in
     1853 was 1,853

22 E.M. Little, (1932) p.5

23 Association Medical Journal 1853, 19 August, p.726

24 BMJ. 1857, 8 August, p.668

25 BMJ. 10 February, 1979. p.431, puts the membership of
     the Association in December 1979 at 62,666

26 See L. Dopson, (1971) p.127

27 Annual Report of Council 1950-51, BMJ (supp) Vol.1
     March 31, 1951, p.121

28 G. Forsythe, "United Kingdom", in Health Service
     Prospects: An International Survey, edited by I. Douglas-
     Wilson and G. McLachlon.

29 Annual Report of Council 1950-51, op.cit., p.121

30 G. Forsythe, (1973) p.3

31 Annual Report of Council 1978-9 BMJ, Vol.1 1979

32 Ibid.p.22

33 H. Eckstein (1960) p.45 BMJ Vol.1, 24 March 1979, p.835

34 See R.A. Thistlewaite, (1973)

35 Lilian Power, (1972)

36 The MPU "claims" 5,000 members (Guardian, Friday 10
     November 1972), The GPA estimate about 3,000 members,
     (interview with the National Secretary, Dr. Quest), the
     JDHA estimate about 5,000 (The Observer, 2 November
     1975), and the HSCA have no more than 5,000 (I am
     informed by the HSCA that in June 1975, their membership
     was 4,980)

37 G. Forsythe, (1966) p.7

38 P. Vaughan, (1957) p.xiii

39 In this context David L Shapiro, (1971) p.103-8 notes
     "No model of public investment is complete without
     introducing the effects of the interaction between
     pressure groups and agency officials."

In presenting this interpretative history of the BMA it is convenient to deal with three sub-periods: 1832-1900; 1900-1950; and 1950 to the early 1970's.

The first period 1832-1900 was one in which the 'professionalization' of medical practise appeared the dominant objective for the BMA.   The Association's first task was to install some organisation and control over the supply of medical practitioners' services in the UK.   Reform of medical education; the institution of a code of ethics and the establishment of a controlling body; the protection by law against unqualified competitors were high on the list of priorities. (1)

The second period 1900-1950 was one in which the Association acquired political maturity.   The acquisition was certainly not painless, but far from the Association being reluctantly drawn into the political arena it will be argued that the Association welcomed the development. Contrary to popular belief that the encroachment of the medical market was a development counter to the desires of the Association, the argument is presented that this was in effect in accordance with the Association's best interests. (2)

Finally attention is focused on the period 1950 to 1970. Here the theme is the influence which state medicine exerts on the Association and the medical profession.   More recent examples are given in later chapters to illustrate the predictions which emerge from the hypothesis drawn from this analysis.   Whilst the influence of the BMA on the NHS is well documented this reciprocal influence has tended to have been neglected.

2.1   1832-1900   THE ORIGINS OF THE BMA

"Everything now conspires to make this present a fit time to begin our great experiment", remarked Charles Hastings as he proposed the establishment of the Provincial Medical and Surgical Association. (3)   One is left to wonder just how aware he really was of the validity of this statement. For it was no accident that this era was to mark not only the birth of the BMA, but also that of many other nationwide associations.   The Institute of Civil Engineers (1825), the Royal Institute of British Architects (1834), the Royal Society of British Artists (1823), the Royal Geographical Society (1830) and many others were all products of this period.   Unquestionably conditions in society favoured the establishment of associations.

It is by no means a coincidence that the era which witnessed the birth of so many national associations was also the period which saw marked improvement in communication and transport systems. The coaching network was highly developed and the railways were about to expand, e.g. the opening of the Liverpool to Manchester line in 1830 and the Birmingham to London line in 1838. The penny post was to be introduced in 1839 and to be followed by the development of electric telegraph. (4)   Such innovations were clearly essential, and as Stern (1964) points out, it was only in the 1840's that any national trade union was able to maintain its existence for longer than six years.

Political changes, as well as improvements in communications, pervade the 1830's. It was significant that it was in the year of 1832 that the first Parliamentary Reform Act was passed.

Clark (1966) notes that:

"The Reform Act of 1832 altered not the powers of Parliament or its ways of doing business, but the electoral system. For the old haphazard arrangements by which many members were chosen by municipal corporations it substituted a national, if still very imperfect, geographical division of constituencies. There was a uniform franchise in the boroughs and also, with a different set of qualifications, in the counties. Roughly speaking this brought large sections of the middle classes into the electorate. It probably gave the vote to many medical men who had never had it before, and now, speaking very roughly again, for the first time the 'doctors', from the London physician with his carriage and pair to the country apothecary with his horse and trap, were political units. There were supposed to be about 30,000 of them. They made a substantial percentage of the 217,000 voters who now joined the former 435,000." (5)

If doctors recognised their existence as a political force they did not witness any obvious appreciation of this in Parliament. The same author notes that the Reform Act

"did not lead to an influx of medical men into the House of Commons. In the first reformed Parliament there was no physician and the only surgeon was the radical Joseph Hume.....He did not take an interest in medical matters....." (6)

There may then be grounds for arguing that medical men, resenting their under-representation in Parliament, hoped to exercise their political force through an association which would exert influence on Parliament. Certainly evidence suggests disillusionment with the state of representation inside Parliament. Mapother (1868) commented:

"No impartial man could deny the importance of having members of the medical profession, who could be consulted on the numerous questions relating to public health to be discussed. The other learned professions are most amply represented in both the upper and lower houses, for instance, over 100 members of Parliament are practising Barristers, and no just reason has or probably can be adduced why medicine should not enjoy similar invaluable privileges." (7)

It is clear that the medical profession was particularly scantily represented in Parliament. In the Commons of 1832 there were 51 army officers, 12 naval officers, 5 higher lawyers, and only 1 medical man. By 1868 the position had only slightly improved, with 41 army officers, 4 naval officers, 22 higher lawyers and 5 doctors. By 1885, there were 12 medical men, 35 army officers, 7 naval officers and 34 higher lawyers. (8) The army and the navy were both accused by the profession of exploiting medical practitioners, while the Guardians of the Poor Law, which was introduced in 1834, were to be looked upon as ruthless task-masters of the profession. How important it would soon become to have influence in or on Parliament.

The early nineteenth century not only saw an awakening of political awareness, but also throughout the country, witnessed a keener emphasis of the importance of education. Wide interest could be seen in adult education. In 1825, for example, Lord Brougham founded his Society for the Diffusion of Useful Knowledge. Also the Annual Report for 1831 of the Yorkshire Philosophical Society contained a suggestion for a British Association for the Advancement of Science. In the medical world this period was one of great changes in education and research. New diagnostic instruments were developed, e.g. the stethoscope was invented in 1819. There was a new interest in anatomy and the advantages of dissection of corpses was realised. New fields were opened up, e.g. the study of bones, the eyes and ears. Most important was that scientific approaches were being applied to medicine and empirical research challenged old abstract ideas. Newman (1957) was to regard this period as "one of the most notable since that of Harvey to Newton." (9) The attention paid to medical diagnosis in the early nineteenth century was to lead to the importance of clinical and laboratory diagnosis in the latter part of the century.

It is interesting that the BMA began as a provincial association and that the provinces were at this time experiencing an unusual expansion of medical schools. The Mount Street School in Manchester, set up in 1814, was the first school of anatomy and medicine outside London, Oxford and Cambridge. Other schools quickly followed, e.g. at Liverpool, Leeds and Birmingham. These schools were to challenge the authority of the London colleges. For example, the Royal College of Surgeons insisted on a compulsory period of training at London. The provincial schools

disputed this requirement. The ensuing battle led to a
Select Committee on Medical Education in 1834, and finally
in August 1839 the Royal College dropped its requirement.(10)
The Provincial Medical and Surgical Association can be seen
to typify this interest in education in the provinces. Its
objectives on formation call for the "maintenance of the
honour and respectability of the profession", and laid
heavy weight on the increase of medical knowledge, the
investigation of diseases and the collection of information
(11).

Little (1932) has argued that from the moment that The
Lancet had constituted itself, ie..1832, it was obvious that
a body of men felt they belonged to a profession. In fact
Hastings in the early 1830's made frequent reference to the
expression "medical profession" although this had no legal
validity as such for the following twenty-six years.

It would be wrong, however, to suggest that the profession
was one solid unit at this time. The distinction between
the physician, the surgeon and the apothecary was still a
meaningful one. In general the physician was responsible
for internal medicine, the surgeon for external treatment,
while the apothecary prescribed drugs. (12)   The physician
stemmed from a higher social background and looked for his
qualification status to the Royal College of Physicians of
London. A charter during the reign of Henry VIII
necessitated the possession of a licence from the College
to practise physic within seven miles of London, and an
extra licence to practise outside of London. (13)   The
Edinburgh Royal College of Physicians and the King's and
Queen's College of Physicians in Ireland had similar
licensing prerogatives within their respective countries.
The separation of physic and surgery stemming from the
Edict of Tours (1150), for many years had left the practice
of surgery to the more humble pursuits of the barbers.
However, by 1800, surgeons' status had risen and indeed they
had their own Royal College of Surgeons of London. The
apothecary, on the other hand, was decidedly from the lower
middle, or shopkeeper class. Yet he too had a separate
licensing body, i.e. the London Society of Apothecaries.
In 1815 this Society attained the right to restrict the
practise of pharmacy to its licentiates throughout England,
as well as the right to charge for medical advice. (14)

Even so, while this description would still be applicable
at the beginning of the nineteenth century, it would be
wrong to dismiss the changes which were occurring. Changes
in medical education, i.e. the observation of the fact that
the advancement of physic went hand in hand with that of
surgery, also the demands of a growing urban middle class
called forth a practitioner who was a blend of the three
sections of the profession. The skills of physician,   ,
surgeon and apothecary were to be required in one individual,
i.e. the general practitioner. (15)   The use of the term
"general practitioner" may be traced to the 1820's and was
common in the 1860's. (16)   His frock coat and top-hat

were soon to symbolise the medical profession. (17)

While the growth of the general practitioner brought a greater degree of uniformity to the profession, the development of specialities was in its earliest stage even in the late nineteenth century. It was the case that some fields of specialism had been contemplated before the birth of the BMA, e.g. Moorfield's Eye Hospital in London had been set up in 1804. Yet at this time within the profession there was some suspicion of these new fields. Stevens (1966) points out that as late as 1860 a surgeon of the staff of St. Mary's Hospital, London was forced to resign for simultaneously accepting an appointment at St Peter's Hospital for the Stone because of the low opinion in which the latter was held. (18) Sir Heneage Ogilvie commented in 1953 that, at the end of the nineteenth century, "There was no essential separation between the doctor who looked after the patient at home and the doctor who looked after him in hospital ..... Practitioners were seeing the same cases using the same methods of investigation". (19)

It would be fair therefore to comment that the profession enjoyed a greater degree of homogeneity than had been the case before or that would be the case later. Of rising importance in the profession were the general practitioners, and this section of the profession found itself without a direct spokesman. The attitude of the Royal Colleges may well be typified by the statement of the Royal College of Surgeons, i.e. that "The College of Surgeons is not, and never professed to be representatives of the general practitioner." (20)

It is apparent that this section of the profession called for a spokesman. The prestigious societies of London were slow to welcome the GP, and with the growth of their numbers throughout the provinces, it is perhaps understandable that the champion of the GP should be an off-spring of the provinces.

It would be a mistake to argue however, that the meeting on Thursday July 19th, 1832, at Worcester was one automatically destined for success. Why, one might ask, did earlier provincial societies not develop into "the voice" of the profession? It would be unfair to belittle the skill of the early founders in explaining the successful establishment of the Provincial Medical and Surgical Association. Charles Hastings proved a man eminently suited for a venture of this sort. (21) He had a history of personal involvement in medical associations both at Edinburgh and Worcester before 1832. He did not rush into the ambitious plan of setting up an association for the provinces without careful preparation. The feelings and needs of the profession were unearthed through the response he found to the journal, The Midland Medical and Surgical Reporter. It was through this journal that Hastings made many contacts and indeed advertised the inauguration of the PMSA. The Reporter ran into sixteen issues before it ended in May 1832, and made way for the formation of the society.

In his venture Hastings possessed what appears to have been the ideal combination of ambition and caution. Ambition may be seen in the fact that while many societies were established with a view to serving localities, e.g. 1832 the York Medical Society, the PMSA would begin with a view to represent the provinces as a whole. It was no idle boast, either. For, while contemporaries may have scorned them, (22), the PMSA began the virtually unprecedented policy of holding their Annual General Meeting in different centres throughout the Provinces. For example, in 1833 it met at Bristol, in 1834 at Birmingham, in 1835 at Oxford. The effect was to advertise the association throughout the country. Branches were then to be created, and often existing local medical societies became branches of the PMSA, e.g. the Taunton and West Somerset Medical Association in 1844. (23)

There can be little doubt as to the value of the publication and distribution of the Association's journal. It carried information of medical developments as well as news of the Association. Hardy (1901) stressed its importance to members. Also Charles Hastings was very careful to diplomatically ensure that the PMSA did everything it could to speak on behalf of all the profession, and as little as possible to split the profession. For example, while the Royal Colleges took up a non possumus attitude towards the plight of doctors working within the Poor Law, the PMSA began in 1835 to campaign on their behalf.

More than this, however, there were issues which by the mid-nineteenth century were the concern of the whole profession. Reform of medical education and quackery were aggravations which united the profession and, in dealing with these, Hastings most clearly revealed his powers of diplomacy. The struggle for medical reform not only displayed the political influence of the PMSA, but it was also to prove of vital importance in influencing the status and homogeneity of the profession. Hence it is worth pausing to consider the question further.

The question of reform of medical education in the mid-nineteenth century was one which encompassed at least two pressing issues. The first of these was the position of the rights of unqualified practitioners to practice. In a period when there was a pronounced interest in medical education, it seems hardly surprising that interest in the competition from the uneducated should also be stimulated. In 1805 Dr. Edward Harrison reported the result of an inquiry which had been made into the state of medical practice in the county of Lincolnshire for the Lincolnshire Benevolent Medical Society. He found that quacks exceeded medical practitioners in the ratio of nine to one. The 1841 Census showed 33,339 persons practising one or more branch of medicine, but the Medical Directory of 1853 showed only 11,808 qualified. The Medical Times and Gazette in 1853 brought notice to the fact that the estimated number of unqualified doctors was double that of the qualified. Another estimate in quackery in 1851 had enumerated 21,400 unqualified practitioners. However, what was probably most alarming of all was that in 1841 it became known that out of 1,830 candidates for Medical Officer under the Poor Law, 320 had never been examined in medicine, while 233 had not undergone any professional examination at all. (24)

The second though not unrelated issue was the question of the standardisation of education. In the 1830's and 1840's qualification in medicine could be acquired by choosing from a large number of quite different medical degrees and diplomas which were issued by totally unrelated bodies. There was no consultation on the intrinsic worth of these qualifications and their standard varied widely. For example, examinations for the Licentiate and the Fellowship of the Royal College of Physicians were brief, oral, conducted in Latin and concerned with the classical languages and a few fields of medicine. (25) The important qualification was a degree from Oxford or Cambridge, which was preferred to a degree from continental or Scottish universities. Although, by the end of the eighteenth century, the latter were giving vocational medical education in the newly developed areas of medical science. Graduates of these universities were unable to become more than Licentiates of the Royal College unless they held an English qualification. There was little or no instruction in any subject at this time at Oxford or Cambridge and especially none in medicine.

The large number of qualifying bodies also possessed different licensing privileges. Charles Hastings, himself, was a practitioner with qualifications from the University of Edinburgh which were not recognised in England. Rivington (1888) described the situation of the early nineteenth century:

"Before the Medical Act of 1858 was passed by Parliament the grossest anomalies prevailed throughout the United Kingdom in the relative position of the Licensing Bodies to each other, and in the privileges of the various orders of Medical Practitioners. England, Ireland and Scotland had different interests. The colleges waged war against the universities, and at the same time were at variance both with the Apothecaries Societies and with each other. Exclusive privileges were possessed by the Medical Corporations and special local jurisdictions in cities and provinces were assigned to them which none could invade without being exposed to a rigorous prosecution." (26)

Such dissension within the profession would be of little value to an association which was establishing itself to represent the profession as a whole. Thus as well as the value of reforming medical education in and of itself, the BMA had a further reason to act in this way. To accomplish

their objectives a unified profession would be most
desirable. For example, the Poor Law Committee of the PMSA
had commented in 1837 that, 'Your Committee are led, by
present occurrences, to regret the want of some general
discipline, some presiding influence over the members of
our profession: an influence which is exercised in every
profession except the medical. It is true that a higher
standard of qualification would ultimately accomplish the
desired end;.....' (27)

There was then the need for medical reform, and the PMSA
with its understanding of the profession and with its
position of influence would become prominent in securing
this reform.(28)   Those who feel the Association was drawn
reluctantly into medical politics would do well to note the
speed and enthusiasm with which the PMSA promoted this
reform. (29)   It was finally in 1858 that a Bill introduced
by W.F. Cowper, and drawn up with the aid of Sir Charles
Hastings, became law. (30)   The struggle proved a long one
and had been delayed as much by the fractious nature of
the various constituents of the medical profession as by
the laissez faire philosophy of Parliament. (31)

The Medical Act of 1858 was a compromise in every sense
of the word. The 21 medical examining and licensing bodies
were left intact and practise by quacks was not prohibited.
However, an over-seeing body was established, i.e. the
General Medical Council, (GMC). It was composed of
seventeen representatives of the universities and medical
corporations, six members nominated by the Crown, and a
President elected from outside the Council. Its task was
firstly, to establish and maintain a Register of those
individuals qualified in medicine. Secondly, to fix and
maintain a minimum standard of education and ethical
behaviour; the achievement of which could determine
qualification for admission and retention on the Register.
Finally, to compile and publish a Pharmacopoeia.
Recognition of the PMSA was made when Sir Charles Hastings
was appointed one of the first nominees of the Crown.

The Act did make a significant distinction between
qualified practitioners and quacks. The latter did not have
the right to refer to himself as a "doctor" of medicine
or medical practitioner. He did not have the right to
recover at law any charges for his services, and he was
unauthorised to certify to statutory documents, e.g. death
certificates. Yet most important in view of the future of
medical services, he was unable to find employment in
government service.

Dissatisfaction still remained however. The profession
did not approve of the lenient treatment of quacks. They
felt that representation of the profession on the General
Medical Council was too small. They also had not achieved
one portal of entry to the profession in that, for example,
a man might practice in medicine, surgery and midwifery
after qualification in only one of these branches. An

20

amendment to the 1858 Act was achieved in 1886. This stipulated that students must qualify in medicine, surgery and midwifery. It also added direct representation for the profession on the General Medical Council. Five members were to be elected by the profession to the GMC and when expedient an additional representative might also be elected by the medical profession. It proved expedient before the turn of the century.

The results of the medical Acts of 1858 and 1886 might be looked at from the viewpoint of the profession and the BMA. The profession as a result of the struggle and the outcome, would become more solidified. (32) The struggle had been a prolonged one. Seventeen Bills had preceded the Act of 1858, and twenty three amending Bills had been introduced before the success of 1886. Parliament had bowed to this pressure and recognition of qualified practitioners had been made; even if in practise there was, as Newman (1957) and Turner (1959) claim, little to choose between the medical skills of the qualified and the non-qualified. (33) The medical profession had, then, taken on some legal identity and also entry to it had been made much more difficult. In fact, prior to the Act, argument had been raised in favour of a lower order of practitioners to meet the needs of the poor and rural population. The BMA however took the position that, "attempts to create an inferior grade of medical men of limited education and with aptitude only for the 'ordinary exigencies' of practice should be resisted."(34)

There was to be an immediate reduction in the numbers of qualified practitioners. The BMJ of 1887 reported:

"From a comparison of the number of names in Churchill's Medical Directory of 1883 and 1885, it appeared that the number of qualified practitioners had increased from 19,947 at the close of 1882 to 21,381 at the close of 1884; this was stated to be equivalent to an increase of rather over 7 per cent. The new edition of the Directory gives the number of practitioners in the United Kingdom as 22,316 at the close of 1886 the increase therefore has been considerably slower and only amounts to a little over 4 per cent. In London the increase has been from 4,564 in 1884 to 4,729 in 1886, or an increase of 3½ per cent, instead of 12 per cent as in the previous period of two years. The increase in the number of practitioners resident abroad is also less considerable; in the last two years the number has been increased by 297, which is equal to about 15 per cent whereas in the previous years it was 404, which was equal to 26½ per cent." (35)

The profession was made more recognisable and its rate of growth was curtailed. With the control over entry, and the growth of prestige of the profession, the social background of entrants was later to become stereotyped. Also over the profession as a whole a disciplining body, i.e. the GMC had been constructed to generate a more ethical code. The BMA was to have a hand in this in that it took upon itself the task of appearing as complainant against professional misconduct of individual doctors. (36) Indeed the GMC's work was to become greatly dependent upon the views of officials of the BMA. Even before 1886 evidence shows that BMA officials enjoyed seats on the GMC, (37) and as will be shown the directly elected membership of the GMC have invariably been BMA nominees.

The whole exercise had been a success for the Association. Admittedly quackery had not been completely outlawed and efforts would still be expended towards this end. However, a distinct identity had been given to the profession and a means of controlling its behaviour had been instituted. Its prestige had risen and membership followed suit. It had taken the BMA forty four years to reach a membership figure as high as 7,000; it would more than double this in the next fifteen years. This, at a time when a steadying influence had been created on the growth of the profession, meant that by 1900 its membership density was as high as 50 per cent of those on the Medical Register.

2.2   1900-1950 ACQUIRING POLITICAL MATURITY

The establishment of a unified profession was undoubtedly a factor which would help the Association in its political-medical work. In such activities two precedents had been established before 1900. The first of these was the willingness on the part of the Association to pursue the interests of all branches of the profession. The second was the success it enjoyed in negotiation with central government authorities as compared with its discussions with private bodies.

The case of the Poor Law doctor was one of the first to interest the PMSA. (38) The Poor Law Amendment Act of 1834 had established an unsympathetic policy towards the poor. They were not to be indulged at the expense of local rate-payers and the Guardians were appointed to ensure financial stringency. Doctors taking appointments under Guardians were in receipt of low stipends for covering large districts. An increasing supply of qualified and unqualified doctors in the early nineteenth century helped to perpetuate this situation. Appointments were eagerly sought by doctors, as a means to supplement their private income, and appointments were made, to the horror of the PMSA, on the basis of a submission of tenders. A large proportion of doctors, at some time or another, took work under the Poor Law, and the Association was determined to correct the evils it saw there.

As early as 1834 the PMSA established a Committee to report on conditions within the Poor Law. Memorials and petitions were brought before the Poor Law Commissioners who had responsibility for the administration of the system as

a whole. In 1842 the Commissioners responded by issuing
the General Medical Regulations and Explanatory Circular
which abolished the system of tendering and insisted that
candidates for posts must be qualified in medicine and
surgery. Districts of Poor Law doctors were limited in size
and some hope was encouraged of an improvement in salaries.
The foundations for the improvement of the system had been
laid and step by step the Provincial Association and the
newly formed Poor Law Medical Officers Association (1846)
would build upon it. This new association had been
instigated in part by the PMSA, and its gratitude was to be
shown in the stress it laid upon Poor Law Doctors being
members of the Provincial Association.

By 1850 the PMSA had widened its net to take up the
struggle of doctors engaged in the armed forces. Petitions
again met with success when in 1858 a new set of Army
Medical Regulations materially improved the position of
medical men and the standard of medical recruits. Combatant
officers disliked this promotion of Medical Staff, and
strove to restore the status position between them. By 1861
pressure from the Horse Guards and from the Admiralty led
to a new set of regulations which reduced the relative ranks
of medical men. The PMSA (now the BMA) rose to the
challenge and as part of their campaign canvassed medical
schools in an attempt to cut the supply of recruits to the
army. A semi-official attack on the Association was made
in the Army and Navy Gazette on the grounds that it had
deprived the army of medical officers. (39)   By 1879 the
BMA had again ameliorated conditions of medical men and
by 1898 it fulfilled its objectives when the Government
established the Royal Army Medical Corps and accorded its
officers military titles.

The success in negotiations over army medical staff was
reflected in discussions with the Admiralty. In 1875,
after a series of memorials and deputations, the Admiralty
issued a new warrant dealing with the medical department of
the navy. Among the concessions made was the conferment
of wardroom rank and wardroom privileges to all medical
officers, whatever their seniority. Later in the 1880's
the BMA achieved some success with the Board of Trade which
ameliorated conditions for ship's surgeons, and forced
shipping companies to exercise greater care in their
selection of suitable persons.

It was clearly through negotiation with government
agencies that the BMA was proving successful. This is
probably no better illustrated than in its early activity
in public health services. For example, it succeeded in
its early advocacy of compulsory vaccination. Later,
besides exacting for vaccination officers a better scale of
fees and other advantages, it succeeded in modifying bills
which would have had the effect of practically putting an
end to compulsory vaccination. It also succeeded in getting
metropolitan medical officers of health made whole-time
officers and irremovable from their posts without the

sanction of the Local Government Board. Further, by helping
to obtain for local authorities the right to receive an
Exchequer grant in respect of one-half of any salary they
might decide to pay their medical officers of health, they
did much to improve the position of officers of health. The
Association achieved payment of notification of disease, not
only for private practitioners, but also for medical
officers of health, in regard to cases seen by them
privately. In 1910 it petitioned the Local Government Board
to direct that a medical officer of health must receive
three month's notice of the termination of his appointment.
(40) Many other successes can be attributed to the BMA
in this sphere; some being of a defensive nature, e.g. it
was not improbable at one stage that public health work
would be added to the duties of the Poor Law medical
officers without any addition to their pay.

The BMA's work in the private sector had, on the whole,
been more bitter, more prolonged and less successful. (41)
By the turn of the century they had made some headway
against medical aid institutions but had little impact on
the friendly societies. The medical aid institutions were
commercial bodies who offered medical services in return
for regular payments. The Association did not so violently
object when such clubs were operated by doctors themselves.
However it did object to the intervention of the layman who
organised the contracts with patients and employed the
doctor. (For example, in 1892 a medical man in the employ
of one such institution was brought before the GMC on a
charge of unprofessional conduct. The GMC could see
absolutely nothing to criticise, except the difficult
working conditions he had accepted.) Reports into this
general system were drawn up by the Association, and more
pressure brought to bear on the GMC. The results of this
were firstly that those doctors who worked for institutions
which canvassed and mass advertised were regarded as guilty
of professional misconduct. Secondly, those doctors who
worked for institutions which employed non-qualified medical
practitioners again were professionally misbehaving. (42)
By 1900 then some success had been achieved, but its
significance is questionable. In 1911 the Secretary of the
Medical Alliance (of medical aid associations) claimed the
first one had started in 1869 at Preston and that now he
could boast of upwards of 100 of these institutions in the
country. (43)

The other form of contract practice which the Association
felt uneasy about was work with the friendly societies.
They differed from medical aid institutions in that they
offered a number of different services, one being medical
care. It was rare at the beginning of the century that such
medical services should be offered. However, by the 1870's
the provision of the services of a medical practitioner was
more commonplace. By this time the actual number of members
of friendly societies was estimated at 4,000,000. (44)
They offered posts to doctors which were highly sought after,
since, as with Poor Law posts, doctors could use this

24

position to subsidise and to promote their private work.
The Association had isolated successes in certain localities
in modifying the activities of friendly societies, e.g. in
1892 in South Cork. (45)   However, in general, they failed
to have any real impression on the policies which the
societies pursued in the provision of medical benefit.
Representatives of the Association met those of the friendly
societies in 1898. The BMJ in 1914 looked back on that
meeting: "The conferences commenced in 1898, but were not
followed by any material improvement, partly because the
friendly societies, believing that they held the medical
profession in the hollow of their hand, were totally
unwilling to listen to reason - they refused, for instance,
even to consider the question of adopting the principle of
a wage limit....." (46)

Partly as a result of the failure to exert sufficient
influence on these societies the Association began in 1903
an inquiry into the problem of Contract Practice. The
Contract Practice Report of 1905 (47) would lead to a plan
to put the provision of medical services in the profession's
hands. (48)   It was suggested that an organisation, to be
called a "Public Medical Service", be established in every
working class area. These bodies were to be voluntary
associations of medical practitioners. They would settle
on what terms contract practice should be offered in their
locality, and would keep the whole management in their own
hands.   Work on the scheme was begun, but was discontinued
as the National Health Insurance Bill of Lloyd George
occupied more attention.

Enough has been said to suggest that the BMA, far from
being horrified at the prospect of a public medical service
such as the NHI would welcome it. They accepted in
principle some form of contract provision of health for the
lower income classes provided the interests of the doctor
were safeguarded. These interests could not be adequately
safeguarded with the friendly societies providing these
services, but pressure against the government had been much
more successful in the past. Furthermore, the BMA itself
had experienced pressure. At a conference of more radical
local medical societies in 1899 the Association had been
criticised for not adequately fulfilling its role in
political and ethical matters. Demands for the establishment of a new association were only averted by promises to
change the constitution of the BMA and hence enhance its
effectiveness. (49)   The NHI controversy would give the
Association the opportunity to prove itself and rally the
profession to its ranks. (50)   The characteristic caution
of the Association which it had displayed throughout the
nineteenth century, was replaced at this juncture by a
determined attitude. It was not that the Association had
been at last reluctantly drawn into medical politics, it
was that now, possibly more so than at any time before, the
Association recognised a crucial opportunity to achieve its
desires for the profession and to enhance its own position.
Public intervention would be welcomed if the powers of the

friendly societies were reduced, the position of doctors improved, and the dominance of the Association in the profession confirmed. (51)

(i) The National Health Insurance Act 1911-13

Lloyd George's National Insurance Bill, which was introduced in May 1911, was clearly of the greatest importance to the medical profession. For a maximum contribution of fourpence a week, those employed could be insured against sickness, and with the exception of a few special classes, insurance was to be compulsory for those earning less than £160 a year (the income tax level at the time).(52)   The BMA welcomed the Bill in principle as "one of the greatest attempts at social legislation which the present generation has known .. destined to have a profound influence on social welfare and the health of the community." (53)   The BMJ commented as early as June 1911 that "the medical profession start with that kind of prejudice in favour of the idea of national insurance." (54)   However, the BMA strove to improve the conditions of the Bill as far as they affected the profession.

The Bill had been initially drawn up as a result of negotiations between the government, the friendly societies, and the insurance companies. The doctor was to be offered conditions similar to those accepted within the friendly societies. The medical benefits of the Bill were to be administered by the friendly societies, the trade unions, and the larger insurance companies, all of whom were known collectively as Approved Societies. The doctors were given no representation on the administrative bodies, and thus no say in the conduct of the insurance scheme. They were only to be paid six shilling a head for medical attention to insured persons. Also the profession was concerned that there was no limitation by income; anyone could join.

At a meeting of May 31 - June 1 in 1911 Six Cardinal Points were taken as the minimum conditions under which the profession would take service under national health insurance.

These were:-

1. An income limit of £2 a week for the insured; no one earning more could be permitted to receive medical benefit without extra payment to the doctor.
2. Free choice of doctor by the patient, subject to the doctor's consenting to act.
3. Medical and maternity benefits to be administered by the local health insurance committees (not the friendly societies), and all questions of medical discipline to be settled by medical committees composed entirely of doctors.
4. The method of payment in the area of each

insurance committee to be decided by the local profession.

5. Payment should be "adequate"; this later was defined as a capitation fee of eight shillings and sixpence per head per year, excluding the cost of medicine

6. The profession to have adequate representation upon the various administrative bodies of national health insurance.

Of these conditions the first and the fifth were to prove the most difficult. Through the summer free choice of doctor and administration by insurance committees of the medical benefit, although not the maternity benefits, had been guaranteed. Local medical committees, made up entirely of doctors were instituted to handle medical discipline. Doctors might choose their method of remuneration within their locality. On the question of income limit the doctors were placated to some extent by the imposition of £160 maximum income for voluntary insurers, although it was provided that after five years of insurance a contributor might continue as a voluntary insurer, even though his income exceeded that amount. The fee doctors required however was not complied with.

Throughout the summer the BMA had mobilised professional opinion against health insurance. By the autumn however, the concessions made had left medical opinion unsure and unformed. It was at this time that Lloyd George revealed the political ineptitude of the BMA's officials. At the very time that upwards of 27,000 doctors had signed a pledge "not to enter into agreement for giving medical attendance ..... under the bill" (55), Lloyd George offered James Smith Whitaker, Medical Secretary of the Association, an appointment to the joint insurance committee which would administer the scheme. Smith Whitaker placed the decision with the BMA Council and they recommended he accept.

The outcome of this action was that a large section of the profession felt itself betrayed and came out in open revolt against the BMA. To maintain its position as the spokesman of the profession the BMA would now have to overtly show firmness. The outcry against Smith Whitaker's appointment had led the BMA to a position of intransigence. During the first six months of 1912 there was virtually no contact between the government and the profession. Not until June 7, did the Chancellor of the Exchequer meet representatives of the medical profession. With the consent of both parties a well known chartered accountant, Sir William Plender investigated remuneration of British general practitioners. The books of practitioners in six towns, Darwen, Darlington, Dundee, Norwich, St Albans and Cardiff were looked into. The report suggested that the ordinary general practitioners received an average of four shillings and five pence per patient per year. (56) Clearly this was well below the six shillings offered in Lloyd George's scheme. The BMA denounced the validity of the report.

27

Negotiations once more broke down. Lloyd George talked of returning decisions on medical benefit to the friendly societies and indeed of the advantages of a salaried service. While reminding the profession of such threats on the one hand, he also, on the other hand offered in October, a fee of nine shillings per patient per year inclusive of drugs and appliances. This was not equal to the eight shillings and sixpence demanded by the medical association, but it was nevertheless a considerable increase. The intention was to give all doctors a minimum income of seven shillings per patient per year, excluding the cost of drugs. An extra one shilling and sixpence was available for the doctor who supplied drugs, and for treatment of some medical cases the total fee might rise to nine shillings when drugs were supplied. Furthermore the government had suggested that payment for assistants and mileage payment allowances would be made.

On December 21, 1912, at a Special Representative Meeting of the BMA they voted by 11,219 votes to 2,408 to reject the Government's terms. (57)   As Cox (1950) was later to point out this rejection of the scheme at this stage was a catastrophe. The BMA had been influenced not by the rank and file of the profession, but by the well-paid consultant and specialist. The lowly general practitioner stood to gain considerably by the National Insurance Scheme as it stood. The consultants and specialist physicians were not to be affected by the scheme, yet this was the section of the profession which created the pressure on the BMA. They, in particular, had deplored the BMA for allowing Smith Whitaker to take his post in the preceding December and had driven the BMA to a position from which it could not easily back down. One year later they were encouraging the Association to reject the Government's offer. Yet they were the least affected by it. Cox later pointed out that, at the time the vote was taken by the Special Representative Meeting, he had in his possession telegrams from secretaries which showed an affinity on the part of the general practitioners for the scheme.

Lloyd George had apparently recognised this split in the profession even if the BMA had not. He had also prepared for the rejection which the BMA was displaying. He proposed that the four insurance commissions to be set up would hire doctors where they could get them and transfer them into areas needing medical service. However, the general practitioners in their thousands rushed to join the scheme. The National Insurance Gazette for January 11, 1913, noted that 11,000 had already joined. (58)   When the local Insurance Committee advertised for doctors in Bradford, it got three times as many as were needed. The BMA was merely recognising the obvious when, on January 17, it released doctors from their pledge to abstain from service under the Act. Cox remarked in 1923 that the Association had achieved much in determining the terms of doctors under the Act, but had appeared to have lost the fray. The Association had been led "into a humiliating Debacle, when we might have claimed substantial victory." (59)

(ii)   Steps to a National Health Service

The medical profession proved more than happy within the
National Health Insurance Scheme. Financially the position
of the general practitioner was much improved; Gilbert
commented "Lloyd George's Act reversed decisively and
permanently the trend, several decades old, towards a
steadily declining economic position among general
practitioners." (60)

The BMA itself was placated by the willingness of the
insurance commissioners to bring the Association as fully
as possible into the administration of the scheme. By 1933,
the twenty first birthday party of National Health Insurance
was celebrated at a luncheon organised by the BMA with
Lloyd George as the guest of honour. Wounds had healed and
the BMA was gradually mounting pressure for an extension of
the scheme.

The BMA had set its seal of approval on the National
Health Insurance scheme in a memorandum of evidence to the
Royal Commission on National Health Insurance which reported
in 1926. (61)   Both the BMA and other medical and lay
organisations testifying to the Royal Commission recommended
a broad extension of health insurance. Content within the
government sector, the BMA exhorted the American Medical
Association to be encouraged by the fact that "the much
greater experiences of the British Medical Association in
collective negotiation and bargaining indicates that the
power of the organised medical profession reasonably
exercised, is very effective." (62)   In 1930 and in 1938
it issued reports calling for the establishment of a
comprehensive medical service. (63)   The approach of World
War II and the establishment of the new Emergency Medical
Service in 1939, only served to further medical opinion
towards such an end. Strength of feeling within the
profession for an extension of public medical care culminated
in the report of the Medical Planning Commission in 1942.
The Commission, composed of representatives of the British
Medical Association, the Royal Colleges and the Scottish
Medical Corporations set out the aim to render available to
every individual all necessary medical services, both general
and specialist, and both domiciliary and institutional. (64)

Opinion within the profession for a comprehensive medical
service had reached its high tide mark. As the government
strove to act upon it, once more the BMA presented a
desperate struggle to insure doctors' working conditions
within the scheme. The parallels between the introduction
of the National Health Insurance Act and the National Health
Service Act were to be proved complete except for the BMA's
eventual more graceful accession in 1948.

The demands which the profession expressed at the advent of

the National Health Service were:-

1. No full-time salaried service.
2. Freedom to practise without State interference.
3. Freedom for both patient and doctor to choose whether to take part in the service or not.
4. Freedom for the doctor to choose the form and place of his work.
5. Freedom of every registered doctor to take part in the service if he wished.
6. A planned hospital service.
7. Adequate representation on all administrative bodies.

At the outset proposals were being made which were clearly at variance with these aims. The Brown Plan of 1943 made some alarming suggestions with respect to general practitioner services; (65) it proposed a free general practitioner service available to all and preserved the right of the patient to choose his own doctor. Doctors in urban areas at least, would work from health centres and be paid a full-time salary. The services would be controlled by the local health authority who, together with a Central Medical Board, would make appointments to the general practitioner service. Also, although joint health boards were talked about as a temporary measure, it seemed likely that plans for the future held the prospect that hospitals would be unified with general practitioner services under local authorities.

The prospect of a salaried service under the administration of local authorities was more than the profession, particularly the general practitioners, could ever concede to. Gradually as one plan replaced another this was recognised. The Brown Plan was followed by the White Paper of 1944, (66) which in turn was followed by the National Health Service Bill. (67) This Bill was introduced by Aneurin Bevan in 1945, and its structure reflected many concessions made to the profession.

Within the Bill nationalisation was offered as the only viable solution to the hospital reorganisation problem. Consultants and hospital doctors accepted this rather than work under local authorities. They were, of course, also offered special concessions regarding the position of the powerful teaching hospitals. Regional Boards composed of medical and other bodies would undertake, on behalf of the Minister, the general administration and planning of the hospital services in its regions. They would appoint local hospital management committees to carry out the day to day hospital management. Yet the teaching hospitals were excluded from this scheme and not linked regionally with other smaller hospitals. They instead would have direct access to the Minister of Health. Each would be administered by a specially constituted board of governors, and unlike other voluntary hospitals they were allowed to retain their endowments. In short, they were being offered a superior service.

The Bill's recommendations for general practitioner services followed the lines of the 1944 White Paper and the previous plan. Local ad hoc bodies (Local Executive Councils) would be set up and doctors in the localities would be in contract with these bodies. A national Medical Practices Committee would regulate the appointments of doctors and by determining the over-doctored areas attempt to improve the distribution of doctors. It was hoped that a system of health centres would be established. The sale of medical practices would cease and compensation be paid. Local government authorities would retain their existing domiciliary services, including midwifery, maternity and child welfare, home nursing and home help, ambulance service, and other preventative and after-care services. They would also have a duty to provide and to maintain the health centres, in which both specialised clinics and general practitioner clinics might be held. But since their own hospitals would be nationalised, they were to lose all control over hospitals.

The National Health Service Bill then created a tripartite organised structure. To a large extent it was the result of concessions to the groups involved. (68) The local government associations represented by groups such as the County Council Association and the Association Municipal Corporations had lost much by comparison with the Brown Plan. The hospital groups represented by the British Hospitals Association had fallen foul of nationalisation. However, the medical profession, represented in the main by the BMA and Royal Colleges had gained much, e.g. no salaried service for GP's, much less local government control, the removal of hospitals from local government, special treatment for hospitals, seats on administrative bodies. In much the same way then that the strengths and gains of the profession could be compared to the losses of the friendly societies in 1912, once again it might be compared with those of other interested parties in the negotiations surrounding the NHS.

Just as Lloyd George forcefully kept the medical profession uninformed in the introduction of his Bill so also did Aneurin Bevan. He argued that the mandate the party had received should determine the introduction of the Bill, and he would not compromise this by lengthy 'negotiations' with the BMA. The Bill was enacted in November 1946, and the appointed day for introduction was July 5, 1948. It was between these dates that the political skill of Bevan is most notable. As Lloyd George had split the profession in 1912 Bevan divided it in 1946. Resistance to his bill was clearly reduced by the fact that he had "wooed the consultants". (69) There is strong evidence to support the view that the major concessions were made to the consultants. He accorded the teaching hospitals a favourable position administratively, he instituted no disciplinary machinery for consultants (although he did so for general practitioners). He permitted the treatment of private patients for fees in state hospitals (despite backbench criticism from his own Party) and in some of the amendments he accepted in the Commons he was falling in with the wishes of the Royal Colleges. The result of this was, of course, the support of the Royal Colleges when required. For example, after the Act was passed the BMA agreed to negotiate unconditionally. Also, when discussions broke off between the BMA and the Minister, the Royal College of Physicians and the Royal College of Surgeons interceded suggesting to the Minister the appropriate areas of concern in the profession and offering the opportunity to make overtures to the profession.

The areas of concern in the months before the "appointed day" were almost entirely those affecting general practitioners. The BMA suggested that the GP's disapproved of the Medical Practices Committee, the prohibition on the sale of goodwill and practices, and the disciplinary machinery for GPs and the appeal mechanism. Also of concern was Bevan's statement that he favoured a basic salary (£300 a year) as part of the income of general practitioners. This talk of salary incensed the profession and step by step Bevan was made to amend his statement. It was to become the case that the Executive Councils were instructed to make such "fixed payments" only in certain cases: when a general practitioner is starting or when he is disabled. Also legislation was promised to remove the possibility of a salaried service.

Beyond such concessions it was clear that the BMA's cause was hopeless. The Minister was determined to introduce the service on the appointed day and substantial numbers of specialists and hospital staff would join. It was suspected too that a large number of general practitioners would also join. The BMA proceeded with a plebiscite stipulating that if at least 13,000 GPs voted against the Act, then they would continue the struggle in defiance of the law. In fact, only 9,588 GPs were against it though only 8,639 were in favour. (70) Afraid of a similar outcome to that of 1913 the BMA more gracefully accepted the NHS. Yet, while in so doing it realised it did not have sufficient control over the profession to dictate loyalty, it must have been comforting to note that its membership at the end of this dispute comprised over 80 per cent of the profession.

2.3   THE BMA SINCE 1950

If the influence of the BMA and the profession had been of importance in the establishment of a National Health Service in the first half of the 20th century, then it might be argued that more recently this institution has had an important influence on schisms and dissensions in the profession. It is clear from the negotiations of 1944-48 that there was a distinction in the interests of the general practitioners and the consultants. Negotiations of

both sections with one employer had revealed if not
emphasised the differences between them. To some extent
the consultants might be said to have had the better of the
deal in 1949. However, the rivalry of 1948 would be
maintained in the following years. The inevitable
consequence of the NHS was then to emphasise sectional
interests within the profession. The tripartite structure
of the NHS divided general practitioner from hospital
doctor from public medical officer. Questions of
remuneration have stressed the conflict between the GPs and
the hospital doctor, and questions of staffing have more
recently brought junior hospital doctors into conflict
with consultants. Negotiations with one employer have
revealed the willingness of certain sections of the
profession to make its demands, if necessary, at the expense
of other sections.

(a) The General Practitioner and the Consultant

The interests of the GP and the consultant have never been
completely harmonious. Discussions on remuneration since
1948 have served to stress the differences and the
negotiations of 1963-68 have revealed this most bluntly.
The problem of this period arose from the anomalies of the
remuneration mechanism of the GP, but serve to show clearly
the undercurrent of rivalry between these sections.

  Competition between the GP and the hospital consultant
can be traced to the late 19th century. Both parties found
themselves in competition for the prosperous middle class
and the special hospitals established at this time served
to fan the flame. "Many of the cases treated at these
special hospitals are of the most ordinary nature and not
in the least requiring the skill of a specialist, but
could be quite well treated by a general practitioner",
wrote a critic in 1900. (71) Criticism increased with the
establishment in general hospitals of special outpatient
clinics, ostensibly for the destitute and sick, but
utilised by the middle class. The eventual compromise
between GP and consultant was the "referral system'. By
the late 19th century hospital staff who specialised were
acting as consultants to other doctors on cases of
particular interest. At the beginning of the 20th century
almost a third of the outpatients and over a half of the in-
patients seen in the Central London Throat and Ear Hospital
were referred there by other doctors. (72)

  The National Health Insurance Scheme did not affect the
hospitals, but it did affect the relationship between GP
and hospital practice. With the passing of the 1911
Insurance Act, the charitable outpatients' departments
ceased to be a threat to the GP and instead became his ally.
Patients requiring much time and attention could be off-
loaded to these departments and the doctors in densely
populated working class areas could take on large practice
populations with a consequent increase in their income.

33

The National Health Insurance scheme in this way brought
a measure of harmony and unification to the profession.
The NHS however, would have the reverse effect. By
bringing the hospitals within its boundaries, the GP and
hospital doctor found themselves paid by the same body.
Implicitly at first, and then bluntly explicitly the vexed
question of remuneration differentials arose. The first
determination of incomes in the NHS was made by the Spens
Committee of 1946 and 1948, which set out suggested scales
and methods of remuneration for general medical
practitioners and for consultants and specialists. Each
Committee was independently staffed; their conclusions
appeared to have been arrived at independently, and they
were based on the pre-war incomes of each branch rather
than on the desirable future relativity between general and
consultant practice. Figures in the Spens reports
indicated that the consultant might expect to earn almost
twice as much as a GP. (They recommended a median net
income (after practice expenses) for a general practitioner
aged 40 to 50 years of £1,300; a whole time specialist was
to receive a salary of at least £2,500 at about age 40).(73)

The adjustment of this remuneration from 1939 values to
post-war values was to cause contention. For general
practitioners, it was left to Justice Dankwerts to
arbitrate. He decided that a betterment factor of 100 per
cent was appropriate. (The average net income from
all sources of GPs was to be £2,222).

The treatment of the GPs at the hands of Justice
Dankwerts led the consultants to lodge a similar claim with
the Minister of Health. Afraid of automatically linking
rises in income to the cost of living, the Minister of
Health related the increase it gave to the need to safeguard
consultant recruitment and to help restore the balance
between the pay of the two branches. From April 1954, the
consultants' basic scale was increased to the equivalent
of 40 per cent above the Spens figure at the bottom of the
age scale, and 24 per cent at the top - the new scale
being £2,100 to £3,100. Distinction awards, which provided
additional income to one in every three consultants,
remained unchanged. Even so, in terms of the Spens reports,
the difference between GP and consultant incomes had been
considerably reduced. (74)

By 1956 the profession felt that their remuneration should
again be adjusted to compensate for the change in the cost
of living. The Treasury at this time sought to kill this
implication of Spens, i.e. that medical remuneration should
never vary. Thus in response to a BMA claim for an
increase of 25 per cent the government suggested the
establishment of a Royal Commission to conduct an inquiry
into the entire question of doctors' pay in relation to
other professions. The BMA, realising the delay involved,
were against the proposal. However, by agreeing to give
evidence to the Royal Commission, the Royal College of
Physicians again brought the BMA to heel as the BMA would

not relish the thought of no spokesman for the general practitioner. (75)   The Commission did not decide the question of remuneration differentials. It reported in February 1960 and recommended that the average GP income be raised to £2,425 with hospital doctors' salaries raised accordingly. (76)   The most important effects of the Pilkington Commission however, were to establish permanent machinery for the review of doctors' incomes and to attempt to end the dispute over the interpretation of Spens. The medical profession was no longer to be able to automatically claim insulation from inflation. On the other hand, the Commission made it clear that doctors' incomes were not to be used as an instrument for regulating the economy. The threat of a chain reaction through which other incomes might rise as a result of doctors getting more money was not to influence the doctors' case one way or the other. The Review Body recommended by the Pilkington Report and established under the chairmanship of Lord Kindersley, asked that the profession make a single claim on behalf of the whole profession, rather than separate cases for GPs and consultants. Eventually the profession agreed to submit two memoranda: one making out a claim for a general increase the other looking to the question of differentials.

The Review Body made its first report in March 1963, and an across-the-board increase of 14 per cent was to be made effective from April 1965, with the understanding that there be no further increases for three years. (77)   For many general practitioners the 14 per cent increase did not materialise. From the pool for doctors' remuneration deductions were made for payment to general practitioners, e.g. for work as clinical assistants in hospitals. Given the fact that the availability of such work was not even, and that GPs had been receiving a greater amount than allowed for in making the increases, any doctor restricting his work purely to family practice and dependent on the capitation fee found that his income had risen not 14 per cent but only 5 per cent. The amount in the pool to cover practice expenses was hence inadequate, but of course the hospital doctor with no practice expenses had received the full 14 per cent. (78)

At the Annual Meeting in July 1963 the Chairman of the BMA Council warned the majority of indignant GPs of the need for unity. A motion calling for a stronger line to reaffirm the need to upgrade the financial status of family doctors led to a heated debate. Yet disillusionment of the GP with the BMA at this time was reflected in the establishment of the General Practitioners' Association (GPA). Formed in October 1963, and advertised by the weekly newsheet Pulse, it was to grow in membership.

Within the BMA the General Medical Services Committee and the Central Consultants and Specialists Committee, representing GPs and consultants respectively, realised the need for conciliation. The General Medical Services Committee decided to widen its scope of inquiry to the broader problems of general practice, and to prepare a draft report on remuneration. The Central Consultants and Specialists Committee stressed that consultants did not wish to be obstructive and the BMA Council agreed in a statement in November 1963, to reassure the GPs that everything possible was being done on their behalf.

By June 1964, the profession submitted a memorandum to the Review Body. They requested that the pool system be modified to exclude all income except capitation fees and the "loading" or weighting attached to them. They asked for a net income for the GP of £2,765 per year from capitation fees alone, and also that £5 million be set up as a system of awards for seniority. The Review Body in 1965, summed up the situation.

"The Joint Evidence Committee have assured us that the profession's proposals to us ..... are based upon the intrinsic needs of the general practitioner. Not upon envy of the consultant. It would however, be ignoring the realities of the situation not to recognise that for many general practitioners their sense of discontent is sharpened by a comparison of their lot with the lot of hospital doctors, both in respect of remuneration and in respect of conditions of service. It is a fact that many general practitioners attach importance to the proposals .... as a means of bringing their remuneration with those of hospital doctors and specifically of consultants."

And in paragraph 46

"Though we do not question the sincerity of the conviction of general practitioners that remuneration has been seriously inadequate ever since 1948 we find no evidence to support it and do not share it." (79)

The result was that the Review Body awarded a 9 per cent increase adding £5½ million to the cost of the GP services. Furthermore about three-quarters of the £5.5 million would be assigned to new expense schemes; the remainder would be paid as extra capitation fees.

The GMSC demanded that the whole of the £5.5 million should be immediately and unconditionally credited to the pool in respect of capitation fees. Meanwhile the British Medical Guild of the BMA goaded by the militancy of the MPU and GPA collected 18,000 undated resignations from the GPs to be handed to executive councils on July 1st, unless the dispute was settled. The Review Body agreed to the request concerning the £5.5 million and once more the BMA returned to the drawing board to hastily construct further proposals. Work then began on the "Charter for the Family Doctor Service" which was a set of proposals to amend and ameliorate the GPs contractual relationship with the NHS. (80)   The profession's new charter was for

GPs only. (81)   Indeed between 1963 and 1965 all
negotiations centred largely on the problems of GPs. In
terms of the differential it appeared that the GP had in
fact gained under the National Health Service. The original
Spens Committee reports on medical incomes had indicated a
2 to 1 ratio in favour of consultants. By 1965 the
differential had narrowed from 92 per cent to 48 per cent.
(82)

In May 1966, the Review Body (83) gave the GPs an average
net increase of over 30 per cent in a two year period.
Consultants received only 10 per cent though the number
and value of distinction awards was increased. No general
award was made in 1968, but in 1969, the Review Body (84)
made an award backdated to January 1, 1969, to last until
April 1970. Compared with May 1966, the new scales gave
consultants and intermediate grades of hospital staffs
rather more than 8 per cent and junior doctors 13½ per cent
at the bottom and 11½ per cent at the top. For GPs the
increase was about 9 per cent. The Economist commented:
"A GP aged about 50 and accepting round the clock
responsibility will now receive in practice allowances
capitation fees and two seniority payments around £4,700
a year if he has an average list of practitioners. From
this sum have to be subtracted those expenses (perhaps
£1,500) which are not reimbursed directly. To this sum
should be added extra earning from any cervical smears,
vaccination and night visits and warnings from private
practice and local authority and hospital work. So a GPs
pay can compare favourably with that of a consultant whose
scale will now run from £3,370 to £5,275." (85)

In 1970 the Twelfth Kindersley Report (86) broadly
recommended a 30 per cent increase for all doctors and
dentists. The Government argued that part of this increase
should be held up because of the inflationary impact it
might have on the economy by its effect on other
professions. However, they accepted that young doctors
in training were poorly paid for the work they did and
accordingly they were to receive the full 30 per cent.
Senior hospital doctors would have 15 per cent of the award
paid promptly, and general practitioners 20 per cent (which
included an increase in their expense allowance). The
remaining proportion of the Kindersley recommendation, an
amount of some £28 millions, was to be considered by the
Prices and Incomes Board.

The Review Body had no course but to resign at this
challenge by the Government to their independent status.
The BMA did not have the full support of the profession in
order to make the threat of resignation. It realised that
it was futile to expect junior doctors not to pocket the
30 per cent increase in pay or senior doctors and general
practitioners to accept theirs on account. Action such as
was taken was in the form of a refusal to co-operate in
NHS administration and in signing National Insurance Medical
Certificates. However, with a general election and the

establishment of a new Conservative Government measures were
taken to set up a new Review Body under the Chairmanship of
Lord Halsbury. In the first Halsbury report, proposals were
made for overall increases ranging up to 8 per cent, with
the exception that no increase was proposed for the training
grades of hospital staff who received the full award of 30
per cent in 1970. (87)   The BMA accepted this though
pointed out that because the new award was back-dated only
to April 1st, 1971, "the profession other than the training
grades had lost out substantially in respect to the period
April 1970 to April 1971." (88)

By 1972 it is possible to take a look at the movement of
doctors' remuneration between 1960-61 and April, 1971.
During this period there were increases of 83 and 131 per
cent in the average remuneration of hospital doctors and
general medical practitioners respectively. The average
increase for all doctors, weighted according to the numbers
in each category was 106 per cent. The comparable general
increase in salaries in the UK was 102 per cent. (89)
Clearly then, doctors improved their 1960-61 situation,
though the area of improvement was largely in general
practice. Hospital doctors and the consultant in particular
had fallen behind.

In the early years of the NHS the general practitioner
had felt himself to be in the front line against the
unleashed demand which a system of zero-pricing created for
him. The consultant on the other hand was protected within
his hospital. Each consultant was assisted by two full-time
hospital medical practitioners, thirty-five full-time
members of the nursing and midwifery staff, together with
other technical and secretarial staff. (90)   The GP however,
lacked assistants. Surveys found general practitioner
surgeries to be grossly inadequate. J.S. Collings at this
time suggested that there was a "demoralization which can
only accelerate the decline of general practice." (91)
Relations between consultants and GPs were also poor on
a professional basis. In a survey of letters from
specialists to GPs less than 40 per cent informed the GP
that an operation was proposed. (92)

In an attempt to declare themselves equal to the
consultants and specialists the GPs in 1952 founded the
College of General Practitioners. Yet, as Stevens points
out, "Structurally, financially, and educationally, however,
the two branches were still unequal. The primary focus of
the NHS between 1949 and 1961 had, not unnaturally been on
the development of hospitals ....." (93).   The result was,
as had been shown, that GPs became more vocal in the 1960s.
Of course, the turning point came in 1965 with the
implementation of a "new charter" for the general
practitioner. It gave GPs higher capitation fees,
reimbursement for most of the cost of ancillary help, and
additional pay for night and week-end work, for continuing
post-graduate in-service education, for practising in under

doctored areas, and for seniority. Importantly, it also provided financial incentives to physicians to combine into groups and build their own premises. More health centres have been established to facilitate a new pattern of general practice in which teamwork is said to be the main characteristic. Support of medical secretaries, receptionists and filing clerks would prove advantageous. Notably the total number of general practitioners which had been falling for many years, rose in 1969 and again in 1970. (94)

The point is that since the introduction of the NHS the GP became more closely aware of his situation by comparison with the consultant. Both parties were subject to the same employer and relied on the BMA to present their case. It is obvious that during the period surveyed the general practitioner had latterly done notably better than the consultant.

(ii) Junior Hospital Doctors and Consultants

Junior hospital doctors may well have been pleased at the advent of the National Health Service. Prior to the introduction of the NHS, hospital junior staff received their board and lodgings and £50 per annum if they were fortunate; and it automatically followed that access to specialist status involved years of financial sacrifice. (95)   With the introduction of the NHS there were considerable increases in salary and a career structure was imposed on the hospital service where none had existed before. However, the demands of workload within the hospital led to a swelling of the middle ranks. The result was that such ranks worked long hours, had shorter time for training, spent more on routine work and had less prospect of achieving the higher consultant rank.

The Spens Committee of 1946 instituted a distinct career structure in National Health Service hospitals. (96) It envisaged a training ladder of about seven years. This would include one year as a "pre-registration" house officer in medicine and surgery before the doctor's name was admitted to the Medical Register; one further year in a training post as a senior house officer; next a junior registrar post for about two years (at the age of 26 or 27) and eventually a senior registrar or chief assistant for about three years before attaining consultant status. The development of the grade of senior hospital medical officer as a second junior specialist grade somewhat modified this ladder; and at the same time the further tenure grade of junior hospital medical officer was added at about the registrar level. There were thus seven established hospital grades each with its own salary level.

It was expected by young doctors that there would be room at the top for those who chose this training ladder. Initial experience suggested this would be so. In the

first full year of the service (1949-50) the number of
consultants in England and Wales rose by 9 per cent and in
the first three years they rose by a fifth. (97)   Even so,
in prewar terms, the ranks of the middle grades were
becoming excessively swollen. Figures indicate that before
the war there had been more consultants and specialists than
other grades; after the war the situation was reversed. The
regional hospital boards and the boards of governors had
filled staff posts on the basis of immediate need rather
than on the basis of the Spens training ladder.

In October 1950, the Ministry of Health, in an atmosphere of
financial retrenchment, endeavoured to impose central
control. The JHMO grade was made a permanent one. The
recommendation was made to discontinue the appointment of
existing senior registrars in their third and subsequent
years, termination of second and third year registrars, and
an annual review of the performance of registrars and senior
registrars in post. To the relief of the redundant
registrars, the BMA managed to persuade the Ministry to
modify these proposals. (98)   In 1951 the registrar grade
was redesignated as a staffing and not a training grade, and
tenure of a senior registrar post was increased from three
to four years in 1952. Concessions were also made in 1954
for retraining time expired senior registrars on a year to
year basis while looking for jobs. Yet while the
concessions had relieved the misery for the registrars the
problem of medical staffing remained. The build up in the
middle grade continued:

Table 2.1
Percentage Change in Hospital Grades (1949-56) (99)

Grade	Percentage change 1949-56
Consultant	+ 29.8
Senior Hospital Medical Officer	+ 26.2
Senior Registrar	- 24.6
Registrars	+ 68.3
Junior Hospital Medical Officers	+ 47.6
Senior House Officers	+148.5
House Officers	+ 1.8

The number of consultants was limited. Consultants
themselves had two built in and long held disincentives to
expand their rank. First, since hospital beds were a status
symbol, the incumbent was loath to share his allocation of
beds with new appointees. Second, they feared a loss of
private practice, as GPs were more likely to refer patients
to specialists of consultant status.

Despite the fact that there were too many registrars for
the available consultant posts and that lower ranks were
also far too swollen, regional boards were still desperate

for doctors of these ranks. It was the case that they were increasingly filled by overseas doctors.

By 1959 a working party, chaired by Sir Robert Platt, was established to appraise the situation. In 1961 they reported in favour of a "firm" system of hospital staffing i.e. two consultants with adequate supporting staff taking responsibility for some sixty to eighty patients together with emergency duties. Furthermore the committee confirmed the need for greater numbers of consultants. They also redesigned the SHMO to become a Medical Assistant in the hope that the changed name might improve his status. (100)

The Platt report failed to do enough. Abel-Smith and Gales (1964) undertook research on doctor emigration. Amongst many other estimates, they suggested that for each year of the period from January 1955 to July 1962, an average of about 390 British born and trained doctors left Britain and did not return. The interesting feature of this study was that it also gave figures for the last position held in the NHS by the doctors emigrating between 1955 and 1962. More than half of them were hospital doctors in the grade of registrar and below; 7½ per cent were senior registrars; only 1½ per cent were consultants. The authors commented:

> "The commonly held view that the majority of those going abroad are ex-general practitioners is untrue both in total and for doctors resident in each separate country. But unwillingness to enter general practice, or stay in general practice as it exists, under the National Health Service, was nevertheless the most common complaint mentioned by those who responded to our postal questionnaire from Canada and Australia. We could well appreciate the reluctance to enter general practice of those who had spent several years climbing the hierarchy which leads to consultant rank and saw or found no prospects ahead of them. It seemed to us understandable that they preferred to take their specialised skills to somewhere where they could use them rather than to enter the general field several years behind their contemporaries. This was a special problem in the nineteen fifties, which has been described and analysed elsewhere. It is not clear, however, that this problem has been finally resolved as the result of the recommendations of the Platt Committee." (101)

Another study pursued this research to 1968. O. Gish (1971) found that Britain had lost permanently about 7,000 doctors through overseas emigration during the years 1952-68, and that the current annual net loss was about 400 per year. The major reason for this emigration was the lack of desirable promotion opportunities for those in the junior hospital grades. Evidence for this conclusion was to be found not only in anecdote and survey material, but in statistical analysis of the age, occupation and career

structure of the emigrants. What was found to be happening
was that British doctors were emigrating from the upper end
of a hospital training ladder, which should have brought
them a consultancy but didn't, while immigrant doctors were
being funnelled onto the lower end of that same ladder
along with the current output from British medical schools.
The hospital/training/staffing pyramid had been shown to
be too narrow at its upper end to accommodate all those
trying to reach that point.

   Emigration then had clearly demonstrated the
dissatisfaction of junior hospital doctors. They further
registered disillusionment with the activities of the BMA
when in October 1966, the JHDA was formed. Soon after its
formation it recruited a third of the total number of junior
hospital doctors, i.e. some five and a half thousand
members. Its first aim was to try and secure proper
representation for junior hospital doctors within the BMA.
Their leaders were continually elected to the BMA's Hospital
Junior Staffs Group Council, but their proposals for
greater representation were not readily accepted by other
consultants committees. In 1969 at an Annual Representative
Meeting of the BMA such proposals were rejected and
following this the JHDA has taken a more independent line.
It has attempted to bring publicity to the complaints of
junior hospital doctors and to provide evidence in written
form to the Review Body and other government committees.

2.4   AN ASSESSMENT

Within this chapter attention has focused on the history
of the BMA from its formation in 1832 to the early 1970s.
In the early 19th century forces were identified which might
be thought of as generating a greater sense of unity within
the profession. The evolution of the general practitioner
embracing the skills of surgeon, apothecary and physician
was stimulated by the growing middle class and their ever
increasing demand for medical care. The market for which
might be regulated by the institution of professional
registration bodies with significant competitive advantages
provided for those registered. Though the march of
technology would bring specialisation, internal conflict
within the profession was tempered by the institution of
the "referral" system within a national health insurance
scheme. A compromise which might satisfy the interests of
all parties. However, as the medical market experienced
further government intervention, these distinctions would
become more meaningful when analysing group behaviour.

   Clearly the history of the BMA reveals that the fortunes
of the representative association have been much influenced
by the environment in which they have negotiated. In the
early years the obviously greater success they enjoyed in
their discussions with public agencies than with private
bodies, such as the friendly societies, would not prejudice

42

them against the principle of government intervention.
Provided, of course, that such intervention was not to the
detriment of either the independence or financial position
of medical men. As far as the BMA is concerned there was
much to gain. To the extent that they emerged as the voice
of the profession their prestige and influence grew. It
will be argued later that the BMA for many years has
benefited as a result of an "intimate partnership" with the
NHS. This was forged as early as the advent of national
health insurance. Furthermore, the association itself
prospered to the extent that the heralding of government
intervention raised such uncertainties for the future of
the profession that doctors rallied to the BMA. As events
looked as though they might prove of disadvantage to the
profession some kind of unity followed and membership of the
BMA grew.

These factors and the experience of the 19th century might
explain a general favourable disposition to government
activity. But the wider embracement of other sections of
the profession within a state financed health service has
not been totally problem free for the BMA. This is
evidenced in the "ginger groups" which have sprung up to
attempt at the very least to influence BMA policy. While
difficult to be precise one cannot ignore at the very least
the correlation between the emergence of the GPA in 1963
and the ensuing greater emphasis of the BMA on GP conditions;
the Review Body on Doctors' Remuneration improving the lot
of GPs in 1966. Similarly the emergence of the JHDA in
1966 cannot be totally dismissed, for example, when looking
at the gains of junior hospital doctors in 1970. (102)
Indeed such observations have not been overlooked. In 1969
the Regional Hospital Consultants and Specialists
Association was revitalised on a national basis. In 1974
the teaching hospitals asked to join and the name of the
association changed to the Hospital Consultants and
Specialists Association.

In the following chapter the intention is to link themes
which have emerged in this review of the history of the
BMA to the membership trend of the BMA. Inevitably the
obvious starting point is the threat to remuneration and
working conditions and the context in which it is
experienced. Other sets of negotiations concerning
remuneration will be discussed to attempt to discover if it
is uncertainty in this area which mobilises collective
action. Also to the extent that collective action seems to
be related to the degree of homogeneity within the group,
a closer inspection of this aspect of the history of the
profession is suggested. Themes then have been picked out
for deeper analysis. Also question marks have been raised
over accepted analysis. For example, is the goal and policy
mix of the association a collective goal. While non-
excludable between doctors when the goal is attained, it
is hardly the case that one representative goal exists and
that members of an identifiable group will be in any sense
indifferent to the policy of the association.

43

NOTES

1 By 'professionalisation' is meant a process by which
   greater control over medical practice was pursued. See
   H. Wilensky (1964), G. Millerson (1964) and T. Johnson
   (1972) for discussion on what the term does or should
   refer to.
2. E.M. Little (1932) p.327 writes that the BMA was
   "brought up against" the NHI controversy. H. Eckstein
   (1960) p.40-41 comments "From the time of its founding
   until well into the twentieth century, the British
   Medical Association played a part in politics only
   reluctantly." John Rowan Wilson (1966) claims that in
   1911 "the days of innocence were past" as the BMA was
   "called on" to fight Lloyd George
3 Quoted in P. Vaughan (1959)
4 S.W.F. Holloway, "The British Medical Association
   1832-1883" (unpublished)
5 Sir G. Clark (1966) p.680
6 Sir G. Clark (1966) p.681
7 E.D. Mapother (1868) p.7
8 G.D.H. Cole (1955)
9 See Sir Charles Newman (1957)
10 See R. Stevens (1966)
11 E.M. Little (1932)
12 See P. Elliot (1972)
13 Those who possessed Oxford Degrees, however might
   practice
14 S.W.F. Holloway (1964) p.306-314 writes "'The law'
   wrote J.E. Willcock in 1830 'recognises only three
   orders of the medical profession, physicians, surgeons
   and apothecaries'".
15 Demands which had been restricted to the upper stratum
   of society filtered down. Both the physician and the
   apothecaries strove to meet this increased demand of
   the middle classes, with the result that conflict
   between their respective associations was to increase.
   The eventual compromise was the appearance of the
   general practitioner. See T. Johnson (1973)
16 See C. Singer and S.W.F. Holloway (1960)
17 The London and Provincial Medical Directory of 1847
   notes, "The Physician, the Surgeon and the Apothecary
   mark its sub divisions; the law and custom would seem
   distinctly to have defined the position and duties of
   each class. It is needless to observe, however, that
   practically this classification has become almost
   obsolete ..... For whilst Physicians, and Surgeons and
   Apothecaries, appear to be so vitally interested in
   the continuance of useless titles, they really are,
   by the force of a public convenience they cannot
   withstand, being gradually classed into Consulting
   and General Practitioners....."
18 See R. Stevens (1966) p.28
19 Sir H. Ogilvie, BMJ, Vol. 2, 1953, pp.707-9
20 The Lancet, 1845, Vol.1, p.422
21 One biographer of Hastings so links the fortunes of the
   PMSA to the vitality of Hastings that he suggests that

by 1865, one year before Hasting's death, there was a decline in young doctors joining the ranks.
See W.H. McMenemey (1966)

22 The Lancet, 1836-37, Vol. 1, p.252 calls the Association "the migratory provincial medical club."

23 Journals between 1853 and 1870 of percentage membership for counties which had a branch organisation and those that did not. The difference is obvious. Compare Durham with no branch in 1853 and with 4.2 per cent membership with Monmouth which had a branch organisation and 45.6 per cent membership. See P.R. Jones (1976)

24 E.M. Little (1932) p.5

25 P. Elliot (1972) p.30

26 W. Rivington (1888)

27 Association Journal, 1837, p.31

28 In this activity the political understanding of Hastings can be compared with those of George Webster and Thomas Wakely whose rival association failed to appeal to the broad feelings of the profession on this topic

29 On its first anniversary at Bristol representatives of the PMSA described reform as the Association's first aim

30 The Act of 1858 "would never have been passed but for the Association", according to T. Laffan (1888) p.133 (quoted in A.M. Carr Saunders and P. Wilson (1933) p.93)

31 D.L. Cowan (1969) p.33

32 The Lancet rejoiced in the Act and the GMC. "We never before had a collective existence". The Lancet 1858, Vol.2, p.147

33 As late as 1834 membership of the College of Physicians could be obtained (provided that you were an Oxbridge graduate and, of course, Church of England) for 50 guineas and by passing three twenty minute examinations. Sir David Barry in 1834 remarked that the examination could be passed by a man "who is a good classical scholar but knows nothing of surgery, little or nothing of the deceases of women in child birth and nothing of delivering them." See also A.J. Culyer (1975) and B. Abel-Smith (1964)

34 See W.H. McMenemey (1966) and J. Brotherston (1971)

35 BMJ, January 1, 1887, p.34

36 See for example, BMJ, June 6, 1914, p.1253

37 P. Vaughan (1959) p.47

38 The provision of medical services under the Poor Law is dealt with comprehensively by J.L. Brand (1961) and R.G. Hodgkinson (1967)

39 See E.M. Little (1932) p.152

40 See BMJ, June 20, 1914, p.1367-1369

41 H.H. Eckstein (1955) p.348, comments that by the early 1900s "The BMA was far more suspicious of private than of public control."

42 BMJ, July 4, 1914, p.24-25

43 By 1905 at least 12,100 doctors were employed in some form of contract practice, see B.B. Gilbert (1966) p.310

44 See P.H.J.H. Gosden (1961) p.14
45 BMJ, August 31, 1895, p.545
46 BMJ, July 4, 1914, p.25
47 "An Investigation into the Economic Conditions of
    Contract Medical Practice in the United Kingdom",
    BMJ, (Supp) July 22, 1905, p.1-96
48 See BMJ, July 4, 1914, p.25
49 See E.M. Little (1932) p.79
50 In February 1910, the BMJ wrote, "We are thus reduced
    to a dilemma from which most people see no escape
    except by some form .... of State assistance." See
    R.M. Titmus (1959)
51 H. Eckstein, (1964) p.129, wrote "Private
    organisations were far less likely to permit medical
    control over their affairs than public authorities
    and far more likely to administer medical services
    with an eye to economy rather than effective practice.
    Consequently, given the choice between private and
    public administration the BMA, having had a long and
    bitter experience with private arrangements, chose to
    be controlled by the government."
    R.M. Titmus, (1959), p.307, adds that, following the
    intervention of the government into the medical
    market, "With the withdrawal of the working classes,
    club and contract practice collapsed after 1911."
52 The employee paid fourpence, the employer three pence,
    and the State two pence giving the famous "ninepence
    for fourpence" of which Lloyd George was so proud
53 Quoted in J.D. Bray, The Doctors and the Insurance
    Act: A Statement of the Medical Man's Case against
    the Act. (Manchester, 1912)
54 BMJ. (Supp) June 17,1911
55 A Declaration stipulated that the undersigned agreed
    that in the event of the National Health Insurance
    Bill becoming law, I will not enter into any
    agreement for giving medical attendance and treatment
    insured under the Bill, excepting such as shall be
    satisfactory to the medical profession, and in
    accordance with the declared policy of the BMA....."
    See P. Vaughan (1959) pp 202-3
56 Report of Sir William Plender to the Chancellor of
    the Exchequer on the Results of his Investigation
    into Existing Conditions in respect of Medical
    Attendance and Remuneration in Certain Towns, Parl.
    Papers 1912-1913, Vol.78, Quoted in B.B. Gilbert (1966)
57 See J.L. Brand (1965) p.227
58 B.B. Gilbert (1966) p.415
59 A. Cox (1950) p.99
60 B.B. Gilbert (1966) p.440
61 See R. Stevens (1966) p.54
62 BMJ, Vol. 1, 1935, p.365
63 The British Medical Association's Proposals for a
    General Medical Service for the Nation London 1930
    reissued in 1938
64 "Medical Planning Commission Draft Interim Report"
    BMJ, Vol.1, 1942
65 The description of the Brown Plan and ensuing changes

is based on A.J. Willcocks, (1967)

66 A National Health Service Cmnd 6502 (HMSO 1944)
67 A National Health Service Cmnd 6761 (HMSO 1946)
68 See A.J. Willcocks (1967) p.105
69 See A.J. Willcocks (1967) p.70
70 P. Vaughan (1959) p.232
71 See R. Stevens, (1966) p.32
72 See R. Stevens, (1966) p.32
73 Spens Report on General Practitioners, p.12;
   Spens Report on Consultants and Specialists, p.10-12
   Quoted in R. Stevens, (1966) p.129
74 R. Stevens (1966) p.133
75 G. Forsythe, (1966) p.36
76 Royal Commission on Doctors' and Dentists'
   Remuneration 1957-60, Cmnd 939, 1960, London, HMSO
77 Review Body of Doctors' and Densists' Remuneration
   Report, published in the Official Report House of
   Commons March 25, 1963. See BMJ (Supp) 1963, pp 131-3
78 R. Stevens (1966) p.291
79 Review Body of Doctors' and Dentists' Remuneration
   Third, Fourth and Fifth Reports, Cmnd 2535, HMSO
   1965. Quoted in G. Forsythe, (1966) p.152
80 BMJ (Supp) Vol.1, 1965, pp 89-91
81 R. Stevens (1966) p.100
82 R. Stevens (1966) p.318
83 Review Body on Doctors' and Dentists' Remuneration
   Seventh Report, Cmnd 2992, 1966
84 Review Body on Doctors' and Dentists' Remuneration
   Ninth Report, Cmnd 3884, 1969
85 The Economist, February 15, 1969, p.54
86 Review Body on Doctors' and Dentists' Remuneration
   Twelfth Report Cmnd 4352, 1970
87 Report of the Review Body on Doctors' and Dentists'
   Remuneration, Cmnd 4825, 1971
88 BMJ (Supp) July 17, 1971, p.168
89 Report of the Review Body on Doctors' and Dentists'
   Remuneration. Cmnd 5010, 1972, p.14, para.36
90 R. Stevens (1966) p.167
91 J.S. Collings, "General Practice in England Today,
   A Reconnaissance", The Lancet March 25, 1950, pp 555-
   585. A survey can be found in A. Lindsey (1962)
92 R. Stevens (1966) p.165
93 R. Stevens (1966) p.168
94 See Table 56 of the Annual Abstract of Statistics
   London, HMSO
95 G. Forsythe, (1966) p.125
96 Described in R. Stevens (1966) p.139
97 R. Stevens (1966) p.142
98 Described by Eckstein (1960) pp.113-125
99 R. Stevens (1966) p.147
100 Medical Staffing Structure in the Hospital Service
    1961, London, HMSO
101 B. Abel-Smith and K. Gales (1964), p.57
102 See, for example, Review Body on Doctors' and Dentists'
    Remuneration Seventh Report, Cmnd 2992, 1966 and
    Review Body on Doctors' and Dentists' Remuneration
    Twelfth Report, Cmnd 4352, 1970

3 Factors affecting the growth of membership of the BMA

The following graph shows the growth of membership of the
BMA. This has been set against the growth of numbers on
the Medical Register which is the proxy normally used for
the medical profession. (1)   It should be noted however that
figures for BMA membership and numbers on the Medical
Register include overseas doctors. The fall in
proportionate membership in the 1960s is in part explained
by the fall in overseas membership of the BMA as branches
in New Zealand and Australia assumed independence. (2)
Supplementary data will be employed when discussing the
development of the BMA in the UK during the post war period.

If doctors are viewed as potential consumers of the
services of the BMA, and if for the moment problems of
revealing demand for the services of the BMA are ignored, it
should be possible from the history of the BMA to focus
attention on those factors on which the doctors' demand
depends. One might typically expect that demand for
membership may be influenced by the level of income and the
price of the good. Other variables which may also be
important in explaining the demand for BMA membership
include, the growth in the homogeneity of the medical
profession, the existence of a collective threat to the
profession, recognition of the association by the Ministry
of Health, changes in the work environment, advertising
and recruiting campaigns by the Association. Such variables
as these have found prominence in research on the growth of
trade unions and associations. The intention here is to
examine the importance of each to the BMA's growth.
Obviously proxies will have to be employed for certain of
the variables. For example, for the growth of homogeneity
in the workforce one can look to the extent to which
recruitment to the profession has been concentrated from
the middle class. For the existence of a collective threat
one can look to changes in the income of doctors and to
extensions of government activity in the medical market.
Though for some of the variables data may be too weak to
substantiate a precise measure of their importance, it may
still be possible to offer some discussion on their part
in the growth of the BMA.

3.1   DOCTORS' INCOMES

An examination of doctors' incomes and BMA membership might
easily lead to two lines of reasoning. Firstly, that
membership of the BMA may increase as income rises. The
real cost of membership may be falling in such periods and
also individuals may accredit the association for the
prosperity of the profession. (3)   Secondly, that
membership growth is stimulated by falls or threatened
falls in the level of real income. Essentially the

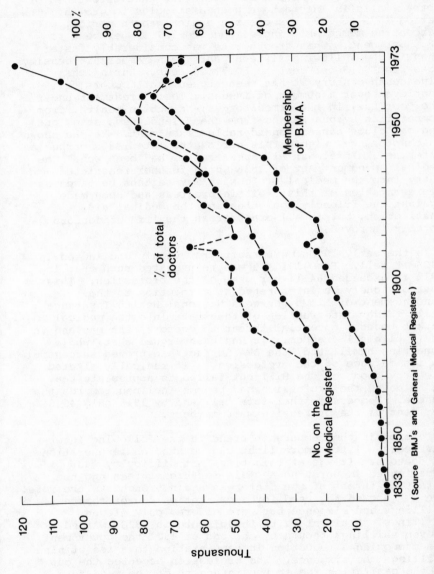

Figure 3.1 Membership of the BMA 1833-1973

(Source BMJ's and General Medical Registers)

Membership of B.M.A.

% of total doctors

No. on the Medical Register

49

reasoning is that it is a feeling of grievance on the part of individuals which leads them to join associations. (4)

Looking at the time series data on the growth of the BMA there appears some reason for believing that threatened or actual falls in income have been a stimulus to growth. The period 1875 to 1890 was clearly a high growth period, with percentage membership increasing from 27.53 per cent to 46.8 per cent. This growth rate was considerably faster than in the following fifteen years when membership density rose from 46.8 per cent to 50.7 per cent. During the nineteenth century it has been argued that doctors felt aggrieved over a number of issues. Their treatment under the Poor Law, in the armed forces, in public health, from competition by quacks and from the friendly societies and medical clubs caused considerable resentment. Yet as shown in chapter two, within this period the late 1880s marked a watershed. In almost all areas relief had been won. The Medical Amendment Act of 1886 which further restricted entry into the medical profession may perhaps be taken as representation of this. Little progress had been made against the friendly societies and the medical aid institution, but in all other areas the life of doctors was notably improved.

In the early 1900s membership grew slowly and indeed in 1908 it fell. From 1910 it was rejuvenated such that in 1912 it exceeded 64.11 per cent of the profession. This must obviously be interpreted as a reaction to the announcement of Lloyd George's National Health Insurance Bill. Wider intervention of the state into the medical market posed a potential threat to doctors' incomes and to their clinical freedom. It has been argued that, while appearing humiliated, the BMA in fact had proved successful in its defence of the profession. It radically altered the provisions of the Bill but failed to appreciate that in so doing the profession had become inclined towards the scheme. Membership therefore fell and by 1918 only 45.5 per cent of the profession were members.

To explain the membership trend in the following inter-war years a little more light can be shed on remuneration of doctors. It was at this time that difficulty was experienced in pursuing a claim for higher fees and the potential threat of the State was again brought to the fore. The BMA argued the need for a capitation fee of thirteen shillings and sixpence but were offered only eleven shillings. Arbitrators to the dispute in 1920 awarded eleven shillings though by the end of 1921 the government was proposing a reduction in remuneration to a fee of nine shillings and sixpence. The profession accepted the cut in the capitation fee in the interests of the need for national economy, but in 1924 the government proposed a further reduction of either eight shillings and sixpence for a period of three years or eight shillings for a period of five years. Agreement could not be reached and after a threat of mass withdrawal of doctors' services the matter was referred to a court of inquiry which finally fixed a fee of nine shillings. This controversy clearly reflects the profession's fears of the monopsonistic powers of the government. It explains why by 1930 the BMAs membership had risen once more to 64.5 per cent.

In the early 1930s the density of membership of the BMA once again fell. This appears strange in view of the fact that in 1931 the government had cut remuneration again by 10 per cent. However it must be noted that in 1934 this cut was reduced to 5 per cent and by 1935 the full rate was restored. Furthermore doctors were beginning to enjoy the increasing value of the pound (e.g. fixed income groups were 50 per cent better off in real terms throughout the 1930s than in, for example, 1920). (5)   While most general practitioners were not well-to-do they were comfortably situated with a net average income in 1936-38 of about £1,000. (6)   Indeed the BMJ in 1939 suggested that conditions in the National Health Insurance scheme were such as to induce a "better class of man" to enter general practice. (7)   In the light of this evidence it would appear that the 1930s gave doctors somewhat less cause for concern and appropriately membership fell off.

The remarkable rise of percentage membership in the 1940s must be related to the prospect of the introduction of the National Health Service after the War.   The government was proposing to take responsibility for 95 per cent of the national market, and this was to affect hospital doctors as well as general practitioners.   If anxiety characterised the profession in 1911 then in 1944 it has been argued that a state of panic would follow proposals such as those of the Brown Plan.   Membership reached an unprecedented 80 per cent of the profession, and interestingly it did not fall off, but continued increasing after the negotiations.   Two explanations might be offered for this.   Firstly, the BMA did not appear humiliated at the end of the struggle, but rather bowed gracefully to the inevitable.   On May 20th 1948, and before the inception of the NHS in July, the BMA Council led by Dr. Guy Dain took note of the 1913 collapse and resolved to accept the NHS.   Secondly, and perhaps of more importance, conditions of remuneration were not fully settled on entry into the NHS.   The reports of the Spens Committees settled the net income of doctors in 1939 values. It would await the Dankwerts Adjudication of 1952 for the "betterment factor" to be settled and for incomes to be settled in post-war values.

In examining the 1950s the BMA has published figures showing membership as a percentage of the total working profession in the UK.   These have been set out in the following Table. (Table 3.1)

Table 3.1

Year	Membership as a % of the total profession in the UK	Membership as a % of the working profession in the UK
1946	N.A.	75 (approx)
1947	75.0	77.5
1948	76.0	78.7
1949	76.0	78.0
1950	77.0	85.0
1951	76.6	85.0
1952	74.0	84.0
1953	72.0	81.0
1954	71.0	80.0
1955	71.0	80.0
1956	71.0	80.0
1957	70.3	79.2
1958	70.2	79.0
1959	70.5	79.3
1960	70.9	N.A.
1961	71.2	N.A.
1962	71.0	N.A.
1963	70.8	N.A.

(Source: British Medical Journals)

Membership density did not fall very quickly in the 1950s, and this period was one when all professions were finding it difficult to maintain their relative income position vis-a-vis salary earners. (8)   The medical profession as a whole found the Dankwert's award eroded by inflation. By 1959, for example, GPs average earnings had increased by 9 per cent but prices had risen by one-third, so reducing the real value of income by about 20 per cent. During this period the community's standard of living, in terms of GNP per head at constant factor cost rose by 22 per cent. (9)   In 1958 the BMJ reported that, "Doctors are united in considering that the Government, by its apparent repudiation of the Spens Report, has broken faith with the profession". (10)   Even so in 1956 general practitioners with the average number of patients (but with no other source of income) were in the highest 2.4 per cent of British income receivers. Sixty seven per cent of doctors answered a Gallup Poll question in June 1956 that if they had the chance to vote again in favour of starting the NHS they would vote in the affirmative. (11)   Clearly then there was discontent at the failure of remuneration to match inflation, but doctors were not bitter about the NHS. Hence therefore the conclusion that BMA membership would fall very slowly. The Royal Commission's Report in 1960 and the Review Body procedure eased doctors concern at

falling behind as against the community as a whole in terms
of remuneration. It has been noted that between 1960-61
and April 1971 the average increase for all doctors,
weighted according to the numbers in each category, was 106
per cent. This compared with an increase in salaries during
the same period of 102 per cent. (12)

By the early 1970s it has been shown that the "ginger
group" strategy had clearly caught on. Many doctors became
both members of the BMA and also one of these sectional
associations, e.g. out of 2,114 replies to a questionnaire
issued by the Regional Hospital Consultants and Specialists
Association, 1,427 answered that they were also members of
the BMA. (13) In 1975 the BMA declared its membership to
be 62.85 per cent of the profession in the UK. (14) It is
fair to suggest that had the nature of the grievances
faced in these years been different this fall may not have
arisen. That is to say that if doctors felt the grievance
to the profession as a whole and not solely to a section of
the profession, those members of the GPA, JHDA and HCSA
who are not members of the BMA would instead have become
members of the BMA.

During the 1970s the sectional fears of the medical
profession have been obvious. In 1974, when negotiating a
new contract with the Department of Health consultants were
made very aware of the Labour Party's retained objective to
phase out pay beds in National Health Service hospitals.
Agitation by the ancillary hospital workers' trade union,
the National Union of Public Employees, brought this
question acutely to the forefront. In 1975 junior hospital
doctors became aggrieved at the manner in which this new
contract was to be priced. Though general medical
practitioners may have expressed solidarity with their
hospital colleagues on these issues it was the hospital
doctors who played the active role of invoking industrial
action, working to contract, to underline their claims. (15)
Indeed in the nature of the disputes the differences
between the hospital doctors were sometimes emphasized.
Noel and Jose Parry draw attention to the fact that the
claims of part-time consultants to be working well beyond
their requirements was questioned in the light of a Junior
Hospital Doctors Survey on the work and commitment of junior
hospital doctors. (16) Clearly these years have emphasized
the threat to individual hospital groups within the
profession and the JHDA and HCSA have become established.
By 1977 the membership of the JHDA was estimated at about
5,500 out of approximately 17,500 junior doctors. The HCSA
experienced a membership rise of 250 per cent between 1972
and 1974 and in 1977 claimed some 5,000 members or 40 per
cent of consultants. (17)

Evidence therefore suggests that the existence of
collective threats induce individuals to join associations.
Initially the BMA was a direct beneficiary of the advent
and growth of state intervention in the medical market.
Ironically the American Medical Association, which might be
viewed as more successful in resisting this trend, has

relied more intensely on the exertion of pressure on individual doctors to ensure high and well-behaved membership. (18) In recent years however the BMA has found difficulties as the problems within the National Health Service have served to exacerbate traditional rivalries in the profession.

In general, over the period as a whole, however, it is also fair to argue that the economic position of doctors has improved together with the membership increase. Routh points to the favourable increase in general practitioners remuneration between 1913/14 and 1960, (19) and the increase in average remuneration in the 1960s has already been referred to. (20)

3.2   GROUP COHESION - THE SOCIAL BACKGROUND OF DOCTORS

The feeling of collective solidarity among doctors may well run much deeper in the profession than just a willingness to protect common goals. The professionalisation of medicine, and the rising status it henceforth enjoyed, have drawn within the profession individuals from a quite narrow spectrum of society. It has been argued that collective identity, prompted by homogeneity in the work force, will explain the growth of associations. (21)   In medicine, it is clear the BMA has grown during a period of increasing homogeneity in the social background of recruits to the medical profession.

In the era prior to the medical acts of 1858 and 1886 doctors emerged from all spectrums of society. Those in the higher classes adopted the position of physician, while the "less well-bred" might entertain the prospect of becoming a surgeon. Even the members of the lower classes of the social strata might, through apprenticeship to an apothecary, have learned something of the art of medicine and later set up practice. Merskey has commented:

"The period in question was a seminal one in English, if not in British Medicine. The basic professional structure, established for more than a century, was changed as a result of many different influences. These included economic and social upheavals, the aftermath of the French Revolution and Napoleonic wars, the rapid growth of the population, increases in the size of the cities, the spread of commerce and, equally with all the rest the development of scientific knowledge. Medicine was a profession in which an able youth could cross social barriers. It attracted extracts from a large range of social classes - from the respectable poor youth who went as an apothecary's apprentice, to the graduate of Oxford or Cambridge from a relatively affluent family - and in the midst of a world in social and intellectual ferment, it underwent vigorous although often bitter developments." (22)

54

With the success of the medical reform movement led by the
BMA this tendency of social integration within medicine was
to end. The requirement of qualifications, dependent on
success in examination, and the increasing length of the
curriculum preceding the examination, was to permit only the
more affluent classes to consider medicine. The fact that
the status of the medical practitioner was rising with the
increasing middle class as patrons, meant that the sons of
the middle classes felt the long training worthwhile. There
remained in the 1880s only one practical means of entry into
the profession for the poorer classes. This relied upon the
system of "covering". Qualified practitioners would build
up large practices by supervising unqualified practitioners.
The unqualified might then learn something of medicine at
very little cost while still receiving a small income.
Eventually they would attend for examination at the medical
colleges of London. Yet this avenue was closed in 1891
when the General Medical Council declared all medical
practitioners guilty of unprofessional conduct if they
engaged in "covering".

The restriction of entry to the profession from the lower
classes meant that in 1944 it was estimated that 80 per
cent of the population (the manual, lower clerical and
distributive workers) were contributing only about 5 per
cent of the nation's doctors. (23) The fact that the state
began to subsidise the costs of a much more expensive
medical training does not appear to have made a great deal
of difference. In 1954 a London medical student paid at
most about 19 per cent of the cost of medical training. (24)
Yet a report in 1955-6 showed that the proportion of
students admitted whose fathers were manual workers was
lower in medicine than any other faculty. For Oxford, this
percentage in medicine was 5 per cent, at Cambridge 6 per
cent, London 13 per cent and for all Universities 15 per
cent. (25)

If there was to be a trend towards taking slightly more
recruits from the lower classes this has recently been
sharply reversed. In 1961, 68.9 per cent of final year
medical students were drawn from the Registrar General's
social classes one and two while only 31.1 per cent were
drawn from combined classes three, four and five. Social
classes one and two make up only 18.3 per cent of the total
while classes three, four and five make up 81.7 per cent.
In the succeeding five years 1962-1966, the balance of
intake altered. Of first year medical students entering in
1966, the proportion drawn from classes one and two had
risen to 74.7 per cent, while social classes three, four and
five had fallen to 24.2 per cent of the intake. (26)

S.P.B. Donnan (1976) undertook a survey of medical students
to determine the changes which had occurred since the 1966
investigation. He quite confidently claimed that a greater
proportion of final year students had fathers from social
classes one or two in 1975 than in 1966. In the surveys
34.1 per cent of final year students were from social

55

class one and 35.7 per cent from social class two in 1966. In 1976 these figures were 40.1 per cent and 39.0 per cent respectively.

The degree of selectivity in the medical profession is perhaps more fully appreciated when it is realised that the Robbins Committee found 59 per cent of all undergraduates in Universities drawn from classes one and two in that year, and this compared with 73 per cent in medical schools. (27) The desire to draw students from the homes of higher social classes seems to be a tradition that has survived the introduction of the grants system. The Royal College of Surgeons suggested for example:

"There has always been a nucleus in medical schools of students from cultural homes.... This nucleus has been responsible for the continued high social prestige of the profession as a learned profession. Medicine would lose immeasurably if the proportion of such students in the future were to be reduced in favour of precocious children who qualify for subsidies from the local authorities and the State purely on examination results." (28)

A trend during the history of the BMA to recruit doctors from a very similar social background was supplemented by a significant rise in the percentage of the profession that have been self-recruited, i.e. that were themselves the sons of doctors. Kelsall (1954) has traced the growth of this phenomenon and compared it with that of other professions. He found, for example, that at Cambridge between 1850 and 1899, 29 per cent of medical students were sons of medical doctors, while between 1937 and 1938 this was 56 per cent. Clearly one factor which may explain the rise in self-recruitment between 1950 and the late 1930s in the case of medicine was the ability to hand on a practice to a son, or to take him into partnership. In a survey, conducted for the academic year 1955-56, it was recorded that 17 per cent of all medical students were the sons of doctors. (29) Research conducted for the Royal Commission on Medical Education showed that in 1966 just over one-fifth of medical students had medical fathers. (30) Donnan's (1976) study gave reason to believe that the proportion of students whose fathers were doctors was lower in 1975 than in 1966, but that the proportion with either parent medically qualified was not significantly different. In 1966 21.2 per cent of first year students had medical fathers and 23.3 per cent had either parent medically qualified. In 1975 these figures were 15.6 per cent and 22.4 per cent respectively.

The nineteenth century marked the culmination of a process which had been apparent in the eighteenth century to exclude women from the emerging medical profession. (31) The twentieth century still bears evidence which could possibly indicate such exclusion. The Todd commission on Medical education condemned quotas for women students in Medical Schools.(32) As such in surveys comparing 1975 with 1966

there was a markedly greater proportion of female students.
(33)

Yet if entry is so restricted, an even greater degree of
common identity is imposed on the entrants during their
education. It is the view of K.A. Hill (1966) that the
"Aim and object of medical education is to educate a student
to become a member of the profession of medicine rather than
a mere scientist or technologist." (34)

The comparative isolation which a medical student
experienced for some six years fostered a social dependence
on and identity with the dominant professional ideology.
Throughout training a knowledge of the ethics and values of
the profession have been imbibed by the student. The
profession has recommended the maintenance of the isolation
of the student. The recommendations of the Royal Commission
on Medical Education for closer integration of the medical
schools with the mainstream of academic life in the
universities were opposed by many teaching hospitals. (35)

The profession then has developed a strong common
identity. (36) The BMA grew up in a tradition of passing
on practices from father to son. Indeed the BMA, and
membership of it, has become a traditional part of the
profession.

3.3   RECOGNITION BY THE MINISTRY OF HEALTH

In analysing membership increases in white collar unions
G.S. Bain (1970) has ascribed great importance to the
attitudes of employers. (37)   Three lines of reasoning
were used to relate union recognition by employers. The
first of these was the belief that white collar workers
identify with management and will reject what management
rejects. The second was the suggestion that membership of
an unrecognised union may become a barrier to promotion.
Thirdly was the argument that recognition by management of
unions will make unions more able to achieve their aims
vis-a-vis remuneration and job regulations.

In looking to the medical profession it seems hardly
likely that the first two lines of argument are applicable.
In the first instance doctors have shown a distrust of lay
interference in their work. Most certainly they do not
identify with lay administrators or managers and, if
anything, resent their potential interference. Secondly,
whilst BMA members and officials do hold positions on
committees within the NHS, there is no evidence that
advancement of a doctor's career was dependent on membership
of the BMA. Nevertheless the third line of reasoning
suggested by Bain may have relevance to the medical
profession. There is within the literature on medical
politics a seminal work whose thesis is that the BMA shares
a unique and "intimate" partnership with the Department
of Health and Social Security in the administration of the

National Health Service, and that, when allowed to flourish
without outside interference, this relationship assists
the BMA in achieving its aims. (38)   Success in
negotiations is, it is argued, directly related to the
degree to which this relationship between the BMA and the
DHSS holds.

H. Eckstein is not unique in pointing to this partnership.
Evidence exists to substantiate the argument that it had
existed since the introduction of the National Health
Insurance Service.   Indeed Dr. Alfrex' Cox, a former medical
secretary of the BMA, noted that the controllers of the
National Health Insurance Commission realised it was in
their interests "to deal with an established organisation
which they believed had learned by experience." (39)
Stevens also draws attention to the way in which the
Ministry of Health rallied to the aid of the BMA. (40)   In
the 1963-65 confusion on remuneration the BMA and its
leaders were under heavy criticism from the profession.   The
Minister of Health (Anthony Barber) intervened to establish
a new working party to deal with the problems of general
practice, and in an open letter to the BMA expressed his
concern over the discontent of general practitioners.   Such
a gesture might be interpreted as an attempt to pacify
general practitioners who at the time were feeling somewhat
betrayed by the BMA.   Stevens commented that in the
situation "the Ministry would be forced to take a stronger
planning initiative both to safeguard general practice and
to reinforce the professional associations whose strength
was essential to running the health service." (41)   More
recently the difficulty which the JHDA and HCSA experienced
in applying for negotiating rights with the DHSS suggests
that partnership with the BMA continues to be valued in the
1970s. (42)

The precise importance of BMA ministry relations is
however questionable.   Eckstein illustrated his argument by
comparing a situation where this relationship flourished
with one where outside interference destroyed it.   In the
early 1950s the Ministry decided to make over 1,000
Registrars redundant and to advise them to accept less
suitable posts.   Discussions between the BMA and the
Ministry led to a step-by-step reversal of this policy so
that in 1954 the number of redundancies was 100 or so.
This success was contrasted with negotiations over the
betterment factor to be applied to doctors' remuneration
set by the Spens Committee.   Here the Ministry was under
the shadow of the Treasury.   Negotiations were to become
deadlocked and Justice Dankwerts and his Working Party
ended the conflict.   Yet whilst Eckstein refers to such
negotiations as unsuccessful, Marmor and Thomas (1972)
are not convinced.   Their argument is that at the end of
the conflict the doctors did get what they wanted.   As a
contrast to Eckstein they see no reason to stress the
precise constitutional setting in explaining the
successfulness of negotiations.   An examination of medical

politics in the UK, the USA and Sweden lead them to present a hypothesis of negotiations which is independent of different institutional settings.

A.J. Willcocks' analysis of negotiations is another which calls into question the value of the BMA-Ministry relations. In his opinion the relative success of the BMA with the Ministry as compared with other pressures is explained simply by the bargaining power of the BMA. He writes:

"the medical profession has, by and large, prospered in its dealings with the Ministry of Health, 'We have the doctors: you want the doctors', one British Medical Association Chairman publicly told the Minister at an Annual Meeting of the Association. 'Crude pressure group stuff' or 'political realities', the Minister could not ignore it and sought to gain peace by compromise." (43)

Surely in explaining the success of the BMA mention should be made of the rate of substitution of doctors for other factors of production, e.g. nurses, technicians; the elasticity of demand for the product; doctors' remuneration as a proportion of total NHS costs. The precise influence of the institutional framework since 1912 is clearly a moot point and as such the extent to which it influences membership recruitment remains uncertain.

3.4   WORK ENVIRONMENT

In discussing the influences of work environment on doctors' behaviour attention focuses on the extent to which their work has become institutionalised. To what extent has the advent of the National Health Service destroyed doctors' status as independent practitioners and bound them to a common code of behaviour? Have rules and regulations been established and standardised such that they have a greater collective awareness? It was a standardisation of working conditions in large scale establishments that Lockwood (1966) used to explain the growth of clerical unions.

It has already been argued that the unifying force that bureaucratisation has engendered in the medical profession is a common revulsion of the concept. Clinical freedom is a concept that doctors prize, and hence standardisation of their work, by the imposition of rules and regulations, particularly by law administrators, is vehemently opposed. Indeed the success of the doctors in resisting such influence from laymen, leads one to doubt that the environment in which they work influences the likelihood that they would join associations.

M.W. Susser and M. Watson (1962) suggest that there is little evidence of a bureaucratic atmosphere within the medical profession. They refer to the profession as "a company of peers in which the most junior may address the most senior as a colleague, and the professional and ethical obligations of the one to the other are fully reciprocal." (44)   Within hospitals "consultants have been free largely to arrange their own work pattern", (45) and are hardly under strict bureaucratic control. Far from Hospital Management Committees exercising undue influence over them it has been suggested that the reverse is the case. (46)

As for general practitioners the NHS has added very few conditions to the life of the GP. In his contract with the executive council he agreed to render all services normally rendered by general practitioners, to keep adequate surgeries and medical record cards, to prescribe on health service prescription forms and to issue statutory certificates. Some constraints are placed on him, e.g. direction of location by the Medical Practices Bureau, checks on excessive prescribing, limits on his list size (though not private practice) but these are hardly sufficient to describe his environment as rigidly bureaucratic. (47)

There is some evidence to suggest that doctors' views have been influenced by their work environment. For example, following the 1944 White Paper on the National Health Service a questionnaire survey was pursued to discover doctors' reaction to the issues at hand. Strength of feeling on issues differed between service doctors, consultants, salaried doctors and general practitioners. The general practitioners showed markedly less enthusiasm on issues such as salaried service; health centres; free and complete hospital service; larger areas for hospital administration. It was claimed that to a large extent familiarity of working within an organisation accounted for the fact that consultants, salaried doctors and service doctors were more willing to accept such proposals than general practitioners. (48) Even so the existing data does not indicate that work environment has influenced the decision to join the BMA. In 1948, for example, it was the case that eight out of ten consultants were members of the BMA (49). This was then typical of the 80 per cent membership of the profession. One might therefore be hesitant on existing data to support the proposition that work environment plays a major part in determining BMA membership.

3.5   ADVERTISING AND RECRUITMENT CAMPAIGNS

Keith Hindell (1962) has suggested that advertising on the part of an association can be instrumental in increasing the size of its membership. Such advertising could take place formally through individual persuasion by an existing member or branch official, or as a result of a particular co-ordinated advertisement drive. Hindell suggests that trade unions have tended to regard the first of these methods to be by far the most important.

There is considerable difficulty in estimating the importance of advertising in the growth of the BMA. If figures in the balance sheet showed the expenditure of the BMA on this activity, or even if the BMJ possessed pages of advertisements, then one might have been able to tentatively suggest the importance of advertising on membership growth. The Organisation Committee made an inquiry into a recruiting effort they were carrying out. (50) This recruiting drive involved addressing letters to groups of non-members, and it appeared that some 10 per cent of doctors thus addressed joined the Association. Of course other factors than the circular may have accounted for this increase in membership.

It would appear fair to suggest, however, that the BMA finds personal persuasion an important part of any recruitment campaign. References in the BMJs of the mid 1960s seem to confirm their faith in this approach. For example, in April 1967 the Chairman of the Organisation Committee expressed his belief that personal contact through the local organisations was the best approach in recruiting new members. (51) In October 1968, Dr. R. Gibson spoke of the need for more personal contact with non-members (52) and the Annual Report of 1967 claimed that "Experience in some divisions has shown clearly that the selective personal approach to non-members is by far the most effective means of recruiting." (53)

3.6 SUBSCRIPTIONS

In looking to the effect of subscription rates on the membership of the BMA one might suggest how many members were deterred by increases in the rate. Resignation figures are available in the BMJ from 1901 to 1966 and from 1919 the resignations withdrawn are also published. In looking to the effect of subscription rate increases it is possible to isolate seven years, 1903, 1913, 1920, 1950, 1953, 1960 and 1966. During these years it would appear that there was an "announcement effect" of the rise in subscriptions. With the exception of 1903 and 1960 resignations doubled as a result of the increase. However, the resignation figure is a very small percentage of the total membership figure. For the seven years quoted it was typically less than 3.5 per cent, and this leads one to discount any great importance to this observation. (54)

AN ASSESSMENT

The history of the BMA provides an interesting basis for analysis of collective action. From the discussion above it would appear that the existence of a well defined group and also a collective threat to the group are of importance in determining the likelihood that a member of that group

61

will join the Association. A growing homogeneity and collective identity within the group and the presence of a collective threat by state intervention in the medical market appeared important to the growth of the BMA.

The existence of a threat to the profession has latterly been seen not simply in terms of the increasing intervention of government. The march of technology and the structure of the NHS has contributed to the development of well specified sub sections in the profession. As Culyer and Cooper note, "since 1948, the gulf between hospital doctors and general practitioners has been widening so that today their respective roles and skills are quite distinct". (55) Since the BMA has represented distinct sections of the profession in negotiations on remuneration and since awards stem from a common paymaster the question of relative treatment has become acute. Whilst doctors feel threatened they may lose under a National Health Service, there is also the threat that one section of the profession may lose as compared with other sub sets.

To identify a collective threat to the medical profession as stimulating collective action has parallels with other studies. One obvious comparison is that of Peacock and Wiseman (1961). In seeking to explain why the ratio of public expenditure to gross national product grew they began by viewing the individual in society as choosing to tax himself to provide public expenditure. An examination of time series data suggested that he was more willing to do so at times of crises, e.g. the advent of world wars. The decision to vote for higher taxes is not identical to that of personally subscribing to associations. Nevertheless both studies suggest greater willingness to engage in collective action. The asymmetry reflected in threat situations is apparent in other circumstances. Willingness to incur the personal costs of voting and in this way pursue collective action has been seen to be influenced by the environment. (56)

While the above analysis is of interest it does beg further consideration. If the BMA represents members in negotiations then any gains it may attain are available to non-members also. The success they may have in defending, or promoting, doctors' interests in this respect is non-excludable. To the extent that they provide this lobby service there appears an obvious incentive for individuals to free ride even though they benefit from the service. Why then do some doctors reveal their demand for services? How readily applicable is this free rider argument to analysis of associations?

NOTES

1   Both H. Eckstein (1960) p.45 and G. Forsythe (1973) p.8
    use this figure as a proxy for the medical profession.
    Note that Figure 3.1 plots observations for five year
    intervals, except in the case of 1912 where membership
    grew significantly.
2   Annual Report of Council 1962-63, BMJ (Supp) May 11,
    1963. p.197; Annual Report of Council 1967-68, BMJ
    (Supp) April 20, 1968. p.91
3   L. Wolman (1936) links the prosperous period of
    business cycles with growth of unions
4   See for example H.B. Davis (1941). J. Shister (1953)
    claims "worker 'dissatisfaction', whether in absolute
    or in relative context has always been emphasised as a
    significant variable in inducing unionisation...."
5   See J. Hogarth (1963) p.30
6   R Stevens (1966) p.57
7   BMJ. Vol.2, p.445, quoted in R. Stevens (1966) p.57
8   John Graham (1965)
9   D.S. Lees (1965) p.62
10 BMJ July 5, 1958, p.20
11 BMJ July 5, 1958, p.20
12 Report of the Review Body on Doctors' and Dentists'
    Remuneration. Cmnd 5010, 1972
13 BMJ (Supp) March 24, 1973, p.88
14 BMJ (Supp) July 26, 1975, p.252
15 The Economist, December 6, 1975, p.18. The picture was
    now all too clear. As N. Parry and J. Parry, (1976)
    p.232, point out, "those who are poorly organised or
    apathetic have not been spontaneously rewarded....."
16 Ibid, p.233
17 Mary Ann Elston (1977) p.50
18 See R.A. Kessel (1958)
19 G. Routh (1965) p.63
20 Rudolf Klein (1973) p.60-61, writes, "At the beginning
    of the twentieth century the position of many general
    practitioners was professionally vulnerable and
    financially precarious. The myth of a golden age of
    medical practice, which contrasts with high social
    prestige and economic status of the doctor in his
    heyday as an independent professional man with his
    fallen state as a NHS employee, tends to apply to the
    many what in fact was true only of the few, certainly
    in economic terms, the position of the average doctor
    has improved - both relatively to other professions
    and absolutely - as the State has taken increasing
    responsibility for the provision of the health service."
21 See for example Irving Berstein (1964); A.A. Blum
    (1968); Guy Routh (1962)
22 H. Merskey (1969) pp 118-121
23 R.M. Titmus (1963) p.162
24 Ibid, p.163
25 Report on an Inquiry into Applications for Admission to
    Universities. R.K. Kelsall, 1957. The results appear
    in R.M. Titmus (1963) p.162 and P. Elliot (1972) p.67-8

26 Report of the Royal Commission on Medical Education
    Cmnd 3569, HMSO, London, 1968 and quoted in J. Robson
    (1973)
27 P. Elliot (1972) p.68
28 Ibid
29 R.K. Kelsall, Report on an Inquiry into Application for
    Admission to Universities
30 Report of the Royal Commission on Medical Education
    Cmnd 3569, Appendix 19
31 N. Parry and J. Parry (1976) p.254. This factor may
    merit considerable importance since women are generally
    accepted to have a lower propensity to join associations
    and unions e.g. see J. Shister (1953); K. Hindell (1962)
    B.C. Roberts (1956); H.A. Clegg (1970)
32 Jane Morton (1974) p.511
33 S.P.B. Donnan (1976)
34 See K.A. Hill (1966) pp 970-3
35 J. Robson (1973)   p.415
36 T. Johnson, (1973) p.217-8, comments that the high
    development of colleagueship within the profession
    "leaves the layman with the feeling of a Kafkalesque
    hero; helpless in the face of professional silence,
    solidarity and ritual. George Bernard Shaw expressed
    this feeling well when he wrote in the Doctor's Dilemma:
    'All the professions are conspicuous against the laity.'"

    Indeed the measure of solidarity within the profession
    in terms of similarity of class background is probably
    an inadequate index, D.S. Lees (1966) refers to the
    difficulty, for example, for a plaintiff to get a
    doctor to testify against the defendant in cases of
    medical negligence.
37 See also K. Prandy (1965)
38 See H. Eckstein (1960)
39 A Cox (1950) p.101
40 R. Stevens (1966)   pp 297-300
41 Ibid p.294
42 Mary Ann Elston (1977) p.40
43 A.J. Willcocks (1967) p.105
44 M.W. Susser and M. Watson (1962) p.159
45 G. Forsythe (1973) p.206
46 See, for example, Guillebaud Committee (1956) Report
    of the Committee of Enquiry into the cost of the
    National Health Service, London, HMSO. G Forsythe
    (1973) p.206; R.H.S. Crossman (1972)
47 R. Klein (1973) p.328 comments that general
    practitioners "are not answerable to anyone (any more
    than consultants in hospitals) for what they do
    provided they do not over prescribe too extravagantly."
48 See H. Eckstein (1959)
49 See R. Stevens (1966) p.89
50 BMJ (Supp) 1968, Vol.1, p.33
51 BMJ (Supp) 28 April 1967, p.28
52 BMJ (Supp),26 October 1968, p.21
53 BMJ (Supp) Annual Report, 6 May 1967, p.68. It is
    worth noting that a personal approach to non members has

always appeared fairly effective. W. Gordon, "Observations on the organisation of the branches of the British Medical Association." BMJ, 21 July 1900. p.150 wrote of the problem of getting new members; "The difficulty was apparently due to want of personal acquaintance with those whom I wished to serve. Men whom I know personally rarely refused to join."

54 John H. Pencavel (1970) examined changes in registered union membership in Britain between 1928 and 1966 and noted that the demand for union membership was relatively unrealistic with respect to the price of union membership.

55 M.H. Cooper and A.J. Culyer, (1971)

56 A similar asymmetry has been noted in terms of voting, i.e. individuals are more ready to incur the costs of voting when they feel under collective threat. See Howard S. Bloom and H. Douglas Price (1975)

4 Collective choice theory and the output of the BMA

4.1 COLLECTIVE GOODS

Whilst the concept of a public or collective good has been familiar in economic literature since the last century, the question of definition still poses problems (1). Paul Samuelson (1954), produced a landmark in the literature by defining public goods in such a fashion that it enabled a clear exposition of the conditions required for their efficient provision. The essence of his definition was that they were goods "which all enjoy in common in the sense that each individual's consumption of such a good leads to no subtraction from any other individual's consumption of that good." (2) They differ then from private goods "whose total can be parcelled out" among individuals with one having less as the others enjoy more. The definition was not beyond criticism. Margolis (1954), for example, found it a poor description of those goods and services provided through the state. Consumption of common public services such as education, hospitals, highways, where capacity limitations are implied means that increased consumption by one individual must be at the expense of others.

Most certainly one of the important contributions of Samuelson's definition has been the interest it has sparked in examining explicitly the properties of such a good. (3) One characteristic said to be implied by the definition is that to which reference has already been made, i.e. impossibility of exclusion. This characteristic is implicit in Samuelson's early definition, since equal consumption is taken to follow where exclusion is impossible. Musgrave notes "social (ie. collective) wants are those wants satisfied by services that must be consumed in equal amounts by all. People who do not pay for the services cannot be excluded from the benefits that result...." (4) The BMA's aims then to this extent are collective. They cannot be denied to those individuals within the profession. Indeed Olson pointed out that any such association pursuing a common aim or goal provides a collective good. His definition of a collective good was quite explicitly, if not uniquely, framed in terms of the impossibility of exclusion: "A common, collective, or public good is defined as any good such that, if any person X_i in a group $X_1, \ldots X_i \ldots, X_n$ consumes it, it cannot feasibly be withheld from the others in that group." (5)

Yet a collective good, as defined by Samuelson implies more than non-price exclusion. It most explicitly calls attention to the attribute of non-rivalness. This characteristic of "equal potential availability" has been the subject of semantic dispute. In the early continental literature it is referred to as indivisibility in

66

consumption. Head (1962) and Buchanan (1968) have referred
to this characteristic as joint supply in consumption, though
objection might be raised because of the confusion this may
generate with Marshallian joint supply of private goods.
Non-rivalness is therefore the term here adopted to refer to
the characteristic that if A is provided with the good then
an identical quality service unit can be made available to
B at no extra cost.

The question must arise as to the relationship of these two
characteristics with each other. To what extent are they
separate entities? It has been forcefully argued by Head
(1962), Shoup (1969) and Peston (1972) that the
characteristics might be thought of as distinct to the
extent that each might hold independently of the other. Thus
it has been proposed on the basis of these characteristics
that a taxonomy of goods might be constructed. At one end
of the taxonomy a purely private good might be thought of as
that which is both rival and exclusive. One might then
envisage a good which is rival and non-excludable, such as
free access for individuals to roads which are at congestion
level. A good which is, on the other hand both non-rival
and excludable may be a theatrical performance where charges
to the theatre are levied despite the fact that the theatre
is almost empty. Finally, a good which is both non-rival
and non-price exclusive would be a pure public good. The
taxonomy may appear somewhat arbitrary to the extent that
the same 'good' may fall into one category in one set of
circumstances and into another category in other sets.
Clearly the classification of any good is by no means
obvious.

4.2 THE OUTPUT OF THE BMA

The question now arises as to how applicable is the
collective choice literature and the free rider problem to
the BMA? There is an obvious need to examine the good
supplied by the BMA. An enunciation of the goals of the
Association was formally made in 1874. Legally the BMA was
not a trade union (6). In 1874 it was registered as a
limited company, but with a licence of the Board of Trade to
omit the word "limited" from its title. Its Memorandum of
Association contained only one clause of basic significance,
Clause 3, and this reads as follows:

"3. The objects for which the Association is established
     are:
 1   To promote the medical and allied sciences, and
     to maintain the honour and interests of the
     medical profession.
 2   To hold or arrange for the holding of periodical
     meetings of the members of the Association and
     of the medical profession generally.
 3   To circulate such information as may be thought
     desirable by means of a periodical journal, which

shall be the journal of the Association, and by
the occasional publication of transactions or
other papers.

4   To grant sums of money out of the funds of the
     Association for the promotion of the medical and
     allied sciences in such manner as may from time to
     time be determined on.

5   Subject to the provisions of Section 19 of the
     Companies (Consolidation) Act 1908 to purchase, take
     on lease, exchange, hire or otherwise acquire any
     real and personal property and any rights or
     privileges necessary or convenient for the purposes
     of the Association.

6   To sell, improve, manage, develop, lease, mortgage
     dispose of, turn to account or otherwise deal with
     all, or any part of the property of the Association.

7   To borrow any monies required for the purpose of
     the Association upon such terms and upon such
     securities as may be determined.

8   To do all such other lawful things as may be
     incidental or conducive to the promotion or carrying
     out of the foregoing objects or any of them.

Provided that the Association shall not support with its
funds any object, or endeavour to impose on or procure
to be observed by its Members or others any regulation,
restriction, or conditions which if an object of the
Association would make it a trade union." (7)

Of the aims which are enumerated the first is said by the
BMA to be its "prime object". (8) It stands, of course, as
a brilliant example of brevity and comprehension. It covers
in a single phrase everything from scientific, ethical,
socio-medical and educational to medico-political objectives,
and includes by inference the pay and conditions of doctors.
Yet there is little doubt, that as the government has
extended its influence into the medical market, negotiations
over pay and working conditions have become the central
object of the BMA. One of the main conclusions of an
investigation into the BMA by Sir Paul Chambers is precisely
this. Referring to Clause 3 he comments: "Plainly the
Association has for decades regarded the wording as covering
pay negotiations and has acted as though the "trade union"
activity proviso were not there or were no legal bar to its
actions." (9)

Thus whilst not legally a trade union, the BMA by its
actions would appear a trade union. Its history would most
certainly place it within the context of the Webbs' famous
definition of a trade union, and it might be viewed as a
continuous association of doctors "for the purpose of
maintaining or improving the conditions of their working
lives". (10) The position was only formally recognised
following the 1974 Trade Union and Labour Relations Act
(which followed the repeal of the 1971 Industrial Relations
Act). The BMA was obliged to register as an independent
trade union in order to gain protection by law in any action

it might take as a trade union, as well as to obtain those benefits accorded to trade unions. (11)

It is clear that the main objective of the BMA is to improve conditions for the medical profession, and in this context working conditions and remuneration for the profession would seem to be its pre-occupation. It is therefore an association which provides a service for a well defined group of individuals, i.e. those individuals who are on the Medical Register. It will not be contended that the effect of the activity of the BMA does not extend beyond this group. Certainly those individuals who require medical care will be affected by the influence which the BMA exerts on the conditions of supply of medical care. This effect however is a spillover, or externality, to the main aim of the BMA, and it can take the form of an external economy or external diseconomy. It is an activity which enters into the utility function of the community outside the medical profession. However there is no direct way in which any individual outside the profession can modify or internalise this external effect. Membership of the Association is not open to such individuals. Indirectly internalisation of the external effect may arise as a result of bargaining or persuasion between those affected in the community and the doctors of the BMA. For example, a Patients Association may represent those who are externally affected, but an efficient outcome is constrained if only by the costs of voluntary formation of such an organisation. Thus the activity of the BMA for individuals outside the profession is an externality to the extent that it enters their utility functions and cannot be adequately affected by the price mechanism or bargaining (12). Furthermore, to satisfy the definition of E.J. Mishan (1971), it is an externality to the extent that it is unintended or incidental. This is perhaps more contentious. Certainly there may be a belief that it is the foremost aim of the BMA to improve the welfare of the consumers of medical care. In reply to this one should firstly note the declared aims of the BMA which are quite explicitly laid down in terms of the medical profession. Secondly, one should note the negotiations of the BMA in 1911-13 and 1944-48 which at a time of great upheaval found the BMA concerned entirely with the interests of the doctor and sparing little concern for the patient. Thirdly, and even more obviously, when there is a direct clash between the interests of the patient and the doctor it may be argued that the BMA favours the doctors' interest. (13)

The BMA then, is in business to promote the interests of the profession, mainly in terms of remuneration and working conditions, and any other effect it may have on individuals outside the profession may be viewed as an externality. Just as any trade union or professional association will argue that the ends they are pursuing will promote the good of the general public so also will the BMA. However this effect is a possible consequence of improving the lot of trade union or professional association membership. It is not the direct aim which is to be maximized.

Maximizing, subject to the environment constraints in which it operates, the interests of the medical profession is a collective service provided by the BMA. It is collective in the sense that if one practitioner is made better off as a result of the activity of the BMA then all practitioners will be made better off. The important point is that to enjoy the collective good produced by the BMA a doctor does not require to become a member. If the BMA achieve an increase in the capitation fee of general practitioners who are members, then non-member general practitioners must also profit from exactly this amount of increase in their capitation fee. If the BMA succeed in making entry into the profession more difficult, then any economic rent which may be earned by its membership is also open to non-members already within the profession. If the BMA succeed in keeping its membership free of lay inter-ference of local or central government then non-members are also protected. Membership of the BMA is not a pre-requisite for consuming the primary service of the BMA. Given the legal and institutional framework, non-member doctors of the BMA cannot be excluded when the BMA maximizes the wellbeing of the profession.

At this point two observations need to be made. Firstly it is conceivable that this representative role of the BMA might be restricted to members only. John Burton (1978) makes the point with respect to the bargaining output of trade unions. Of this activity he argues that exclusion is both technically and economically feasible if trade unions bargain and enforce contracts on behalf of their own members, leaving non-members to negotiate and enforce their own bargains. In the USA section 9 (a) of the Wagner Act requires that "representatives designated by ..... the majority of employees in a unit .... shall be the exclusive representatives of all employees in such a unit for the purpose of collective bargaining". It is in this case arguable that the law has artificially created a collective good problem. The observation is in keeping with the work of other authors such as Coase (1974), who indicates how property rights can be established in the provision of lighthouse facilities which stood as the classic example of the pure collective good. Indeed Goldin's (1977) survey indicates clearly the problem of referring to any good as a pure collective good.

This comment on the output of trade unions is clearly of importance. However in the first instance the argument does not stand without question. In instances where the BMA's objective is to raise the social standing and prestige of the medical profession will there not be a collective good problem, except for cases where BMA membership equals membership of the profession? In cases where concern is expressed about, for example, safety and fire precautions in hospitals is it really possible to do so with effect only to BMA members in hospitals? These cases are arguable and whilst exclusion techniques may be eventually established one must be constantly concerned also about the costs they may incur. (14) Yet the general argument, while of considerable interest, does not materially affect the study in hand since evidence suggests that, for whatever reason, BMA negotiation and achievements have been made on behalf of and to the possible benefit of non-members as well as members. Why this has been so is a question to be considered elsewhere. The evidence is then that exclusion has not been effected for this output.

The second point to note when looking at the goals of the Association is, of course, the other kinds of output, e.g. to hold periodically meetings for the members, to circulate information as may be thought desirable by means of a periodical journal. These forms of output may not be classed as private goods though may be, to a greater extent, excludable. These outputs will not be ignored and their effect on membership will be examined. At present, however, the study begins on the premise that some part of the output of the BMA may be classed as a pure collective good.

4.3 THE VOLUNTARY PROVISION OF COLLECTIVE GOODS

Considering a pure collective good as one which is non-rival and non-excludable, the question arises as to the conditions that must hold in order that one might have confidence that it was provided in an optimal fashion. By optimal, reference is generally made to the Pareto criterion, that resources must be allocated in such a fashion that it is impossible to make someone better off without making someone else worse off. The conditions under which this situation holds can be illustrated in Figure 4.1. Here the demand curves for two individuals for the collective good are illustrated. The costs of producing more of the good are constant so that the marginal cost curve is parallel to the horizontal axis. Each individual, A and B consumes the same output so that the aggregate demand D_{A+B} is attained by summing vertically, over price, the willingness to pay for the good. In this partial equilibrium framework, the optimal output is equal to OQ where $OP_A + OP_B = MC$ (15).

Technically the Pareto optimal conditions for the provision of public goods may be specified. However there is considerable doubt that the output level that satisfies these conditions will be that which is attained voluntarily in the market. The likelihood is rather that too little or indeed no output at all will result. Macmillan (1979) refers to both these possibilities within the framework of what is referred to as the "free rider problem".

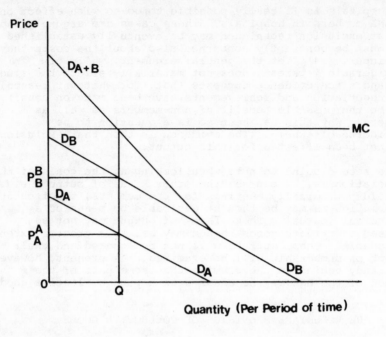

Figure 4.1 Optimal Provision of a Collective Good

If for any individual his marginal evaluation exceeds the costs of the good, then he will provide some output of the good rather than remain in a situation where he is consuming nothing. Such a situation is here depicted in Figure 4.2, where individual B's demand for the good is such that until output OQ_1 he is willing to pay more for the good than it costs to provide the good. In this situation it seems likely that, regardless of the size of the group who will consume the good, output OQ_1 will be forthcoming. The optimal output is OQ_2 and clearly under these conditions the final situation is one of under provision. Furthermore, the situation is said to be one where the individual with the greater demand for the good is bearing a disproportionate share of the costs of providing the good. In effect this must be true as individual A consumes the same output, i.e. OQ_1, at zero cost. As such he enjoys a "free ride".

A solution which is optimal might be attained by a process of 'voluntary exchange.' If bargaining were possible then, in Figure 4.2, if an output of OQ_2 were considered and A

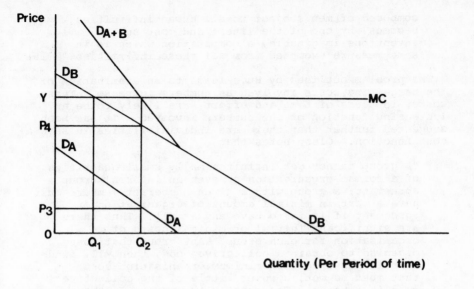

Figure 4.2 Individual Provision of Collective Goods

offered to pay OP_3 per unit, which is equal to his marginal
evaluation of the good, then it is likely that B would be
prepared to pay the remaining amount of P_3Y per unit, for
B's marginal evaluation OP_4 equals P_3Y. In such a situation
a process emerges where such bargaining can lead to a
movement to an output which is optimal.

It is in this context that the question of the number of
individuals involved is of importance. David Hume's
famous example indicates all too clearly the problem.

"......Two neighbours may agree to drain a meadow,
which they possess in common: because it is easy
for them to know each other's mind; and each must
perceive, that the immediate consequence of his
failing in his part, is the abandoning the whole
project. But is is difficult, and indeed impossible,
that a thousand persons should agree in any such
action; it being difficult for them to concert so
complicated a design, and still more difficult for
them to execute it, while each seeks a pretext to
free himself of the trouble and expense, and would
lay the whole burden on others. Political society
easily remedies both these inconveniences..... Thus
bridges are built, harbours opened, ramparts raised,
canals formed, fleets equipped and armies disciplined
everywhere by the care of government, which, though

73

composed of men subject to all human infirmities,
becomes, by one of the finest and most subtle
inventions imaginable, a composition which is in
some measure exempted from all these infirmities." (16)

The problem outlined by Hume leads to an examination of
the bargaining costs involved as numbers increase. These
costs, in terms of time and effort, are likely to be an
increasing function of the numbers involved. It has been
suggested further that there are indivisibilities in such a
cost function. Olson notes that:

"A group cannot get infinitesimally small quantities
of a formal organisation or even an informal group
agreement; a group with a given number of members must
have a certain minimal amount of organisation or
agreement if it is to have any at all. Thus there
are significant initial or minimal costs of
organisation for each group. Any group that must
organise to obtain a collective good, then will find
that it has a certain minimum organisation cost
that must be met, however little of the collective
good it obtains. The greater the number in the
group the greater these minimal costs will be." (17)

However from the point of view of individual participants
one of the most important effects of increasing the size
of the group is that each individual in the group finds
that his contribution to the costs of providing the
collective good becomes less significant. As the size of
the group increases he feels himself to be one of many,
such that his personal contribution may in no significant
fashion increase the likelihood that the good would be
provided. In the case of the small group which has just
been described, past experience will have made both A and
B aware that their contribution is vital to the provision
of any of the good. Yet in the case of the large group
each individual may hope that the sub-set (i.e. everyone
other than himself) could cover the cost. If this outcome
does not occur he may then feel that his own personal
contribution, being one of many, would be ineffective.

The small group is then characterised as one in which
strategic interaction is important. That is the behaviour
of one individual in the small group can effectively alter
the likelihood of any of the public good being provided.
The large group on the other hand is one in which "the
individual does not predict that his own behaviour can
influence others in the group". (18) The individual takes
the environment as given and each individual does not
feel that he can by his own actions affect it. The
distinction is one which is readily used in economics as
between the duopoly or oligopoly situation and perfect
competition.

In the case of the provision of a collective good the

effectiveness of strategic interaction in the small group
can be clearly illustrated in Table 4.1.   Following
Buchanan (1968), assume a small group of individuals wish
to provide themselves with a good. Each individual is
asked to contribute £5 in the hope that a good valued at
£10 by each will be provided. The total cost of the good
however, is well above £10 and hence for its provision
others must contribute.

Table 4.1
The Small Group Situation

	Others Contribute	Others do not contribute	Expected Value
Individual contributes	£5 (0.8)	- £5 (0.2)	£3
Individual does not contribute	£10 (.2)	0 (0.8)	£2

In Table 4.1 it is clear, that if the individual
contributes and others contribute, then he stands to see a
return on his contribution of £5. If he contributes and
others do not, he simply loses his £5. On the other hand,
if he does not contribute and others do, then he receives
the full £10 free of any charge, as the good is non-
excludable. If neither he, nor any others contribute,
then he neither stands to gain nor lose anything. In the
small group case, however, the individual realises that his
contribution is significant to the successful provision of
the good. The probability is 0.8 that if he contributes
then others will respond by making a contribution and the
good will be provided. In such a case, the net expected
value of contributing is greater than that of not
contributing.

Table 4.2
The Large Group Situation

	Others Contribute	Others do not Contribute	Expected Value
Individual contributes	£5 (0.5)	- £5 (0.5)	0
Individual does not contribute	£10 (0.5)	0 (0.5)	£5

In the case of the large group (Table 4.2) the individual does not feel that his contribution is significant. He takes the environment as given and assumes that the chances of others contributing if he contributes is exactly the same as others not contributing when he contributes. With a fifty-fifty chance of others contributing whether or not the individual contributes the expected value of not contributing is greater.

It should be noted that the prediction that the individual will not contribute is very robust. The pay-offs for the strategy of not contributing are everywhere greater than those for contributing and the strategy of not contributing is said to dominate that of contributing. (19) Where a probability of 0.5 is attached to each of the possible outcomes, or whether any other probability is attached to "others contribute", the strategy of not contributing will yield a higher expected value provided that the probability that "others contribute" is not affected by the individual contributing or not contributing.

The application of many decision making rules for conditions of complete uncertainty also support the view that the individual will not participate. For example, where the individual has no idea of which outcome may follow, i.e. "others contribute" or "others do not contribute", one approach to the problem is to pursue a maximin approach. The individual in this way acts cautiously and looks for the worst possible outcome, which in this case is "others do not contribute", and chooses that strategy which leaves him in the best situation should the worst occur. Again the prediction is that he will not contribute. The maximin approach is not the only possibility. An optimist may apply a maximax approach, i.e. choose the strategy which leaves one at the best position should the most favourable outcome ensue. The application of this decision making rule leads to the same prediction. (20).

It is in this way then that the "free-rider" problem can be illustrated. In its strictest form it predicts that individuals will not reveal their demand for the good even though if all individuals contributed they would each benefit from the provision of the good.

It is interesting to note, at this time, that even if the individual was thought altruistic in nature the prediction would not alter. If the individual was asked to give £5 to a "worthy cause", such that when others gave he benefited to the extent of £10 from the attainment of that goal, he still has no incentive to subscribe. (21) As Olson notes, "even if the member of a large group were to neglect his own interests entirely he still would not rationally contribute toward the provision of any collective or public good, since his own contribution would not be perceptible". (22) Indeed unless one can infer any happiness to the donor from the "act" of giving,

independent of the end result, the prediction again appears
one of unwillingness to reveal preferences. (23)

4.4   THE BIRTH OF THE BMA

It might be argued that the origins of the BMA are quite
consistent with the theory of collective choice. Here two
distinctions are important. Firstly, that between the size
of the Association and the size of the group. Secondly,
that between an "inclusive" group and an "exclusive group"
(24).

It has been shown that "in a very small group where each
member gets a substantial proportion of the total gain
simply because there are few others in the group, a
collective good can often be provided by the voluntary self-
interested action of the members of the group". (25) One
argument levelled against large groups is that as the group
becomes larger, given that the good provided is non-exclusive
each individual member of the group will personally receive
less than he did before, and hence the incentive for him to
contribute has been reduced. This conclusion follows if
the benefit received from the good remains evenly
distributed as the group gets larger and also provided that
the total amount of the good consumed remains constant as
the group becomes larger.

It is clear however that an individual can only get less
of the good as numbers increase if that good is rival in
consumption. Here the objective of the group may be to keep
the numbers involved low, e.g. cartels may organise to
restrict entry to a market in order to maintain members'
share. The group in this respect is "exclusive". However
for goods which are non rival this problem does not exist.
A pressure group which seeks to promote some legislative
change may be pursuing such a good and, to the extent that
greater numbers in the association reduces per unit costs,
they may be inclined to attract potential members to their
cause. The group may then be termed "inclusive".

In the case of the "inclusive" group the size of the group
is less debilitating. If within a large group a sub-set
of individuals are particular beneficiaries from the
collective good, and hence incur bargaining costs to provide
some output, their action is not affected if there is one
non member or 100,000 non members. The problem in this
respect then would arise as the costs of providing the good
rise such that a large number in the association is required
to provide any amount. In this respect the problem of
bargaining and of each individual being unable to perceive
the importance of his contribution to the association are
relevant.

In the case of the BMA it may have been that in 1832 a
sub-set of all medical practitioners had a demand for the

services of a professional association, and that for this sub-set of a large group the benefits exceeded the costs. Hastings for example had greater than average interest in medical education reform and in medical research. The licensing laws meant that his qualification from Edinburgh was not valid in parts of England so that he had much to gain by reform of medical education. This was so even though Edinburgh at the time had been one of the most prominent centres for medical research. Also, interestingly, early members such as Hastings and Professor Kidd of Oxford were likely to have higher than average incomes. Hastings had one of the largest practices in Worcestershire. It is not improbable that the demand for the services of a professional association were for this sub-set greater than average. The early costs for this small sub-set may not have been prohibitive and since medical education reform might be looked on as non-rival the group was "inclusive" in the sense that the sub-set would not be necessarily deterred by the number of non-members.

This description of events is clearly speculative. The problem however is why at this present period of time, when association membership is so large and each individual's contribution is virtually imperceptible, do members voluntarily contribute. In the next two chapters two possibilities are pursued. Firstly, that doctors do not have as much choice to join as has been assumed. Secondly, that they join for other services which are contingent on membership.

NOTES

1 See R.A. Musgrave and A.T. Peacock (1967)
2 P.A. Samuelson (1954) (reprinted in Houghton (1970) p.179)
3 See J.G. Head (1962)
4 R.A. Musgrave (1959) p.8
5 M. Olson, Jr.(1971) p.14
6 It has often been described as a trade union, e.g. Prof. H. Laski rather uncomplementarily, as well as somewhat unfairly, referred to it as a "tenth rate trade union" BMJ (Supp) May 11, 1946, p.119
7 BMJ (Supp) May 6, 1972, p.49
8 See for example the statement by Dr. John Happel, who was Chairman of the BMA Ethical Committee "... the first object of the BMA is to preserve the honour and independence of the profession...." The Sunday Times Nov. 30, 1975, p.1
9 BMJ (Supp) May 6, 1972, p.50
10 S & B Webb, (1920) p.1
11 Norman Ellis, "Two views on medical unionism: The BMA as a trade union", BMJ 2 June 1979, pp 1498-9 writes, "until 1975 the BMA retained a restrictive clause in its articles which specifically prevented the Association from pursuing trade union objectives. Whenever the BMA found itself in dispute with

Government over the pay and conditions of service of members, any possible constitutional and legal difficulties were avoided by adopting the guise of the British Medical Guild which was established in 1949 for the purpose of taking union type action."

12 See J.M. Buchanan and W.G. Stubblebine (1962) for a discussion of the definition of an externality. For the distinction between this concept and that of a collective good, see A.W. Evans (1970) and E.J. Mishan (1969)

13 J.L. Brand (1965) commented on the National Health Insurance negotiations:
"The British Medical Association never attempted to introduce any fundamental changes in the Bill which might improve its public health implications. True one provision of the Act (Section 63) dealt with action to be taken in areas where illness among insured persons was revealed. The Association did not, however, attempt to improve the Bill in regard to larger questions of co-ordination with the public health authorities. The Act covered only a segment of the population - almost entirely the adult male wage earner - and then only for short-term risks. Even Lloyd George viewed the legislation as a temporary expedient. The medical benefit did not include major operations, specialist services, nurses, diagnostic X-ray, or general hospital services. The British Medical Journal took note of such weaknesses, but the Association had not seen fit to incorporate them in its "cardinal points".

More forcefully Eckstein (1958) p.125-6, comments on the centenary history by Little (1932)
"the writer of the centenary history could not conceal the fact that the financial interests of the Association's members have always been far in the forefront of its pre-occupations. As a matter of fact a great many of the public health activities on which the BMA now prides its social conscience were pursued at least partly because they promoted these interests. For example, the fight against Poor Law practices, however praiseworthy its result, centred very largely on conditions of practice and doctors' remuneration. The Association battled long and hard against arrangements forcing conscientious doctors to provide their services in effect as charity, due to the parsimony of local Guardians. It insisted on the limitation of districts to be served by District Medical Officers, on adequate qualifications on the part of such officers and on their responsibility to medical authority rather than Relieving Officers and other local bureaucrats. No doubt public benefits accrued from its stand, but that does not mean that public rather than corporate benefit was the Association's aim. The same point applies to the Association's

role in improving the conditions of Medical Officers of Health. And as definitive evidence, consider the Association's position on school and maternity clinics. It was heartily in favour of the schemes, but only up to the point where the profession's corporate interests as predominantly private practitioners were likely to be affected. It favoured school inspections, but it was very much opposed to a full-time, salaried school service, which might seriously decrease private practice. It was all for maternity clinics, but it insisted that they be used simply for education because they were bound to increase the demand for private services while active treatment, in both schools and clinics was bound to diminish it."

14 For a critique on the view that outputs of Associations can easily be made excludable see Ricketts (1978). Bennett and Johnson (1979) take up the related point that a "demand revealing process" might be adopted. This procedure, suggested by Clarke (1971) and developed by Tideman and Tullock (1976), incorporates the use of a tax to provide an incentive for individuals not to under or over reveal preferences for union services. The tax to any individual is related to the net cost of all other persons of adopting the individual's preferred outcome. Again the process is of interest, but not generally identified in the experience of the BMA.

15 Following C.V. Brown and P.M. Jackson, (1978) p.46, the public finance literature reveals alternative expressions for the efficient provision of collective goods. All depends on the assumptions under which the demand curves are drawn. Musgrave favours using the assumption that money income is held constant and expresses the condition for efficiency as Σ individual prices = marginal cost. Bowen (like Samuelson) prefers to hold real income constant and instead of talking about demand curves employ "marginal rate of substitution curves". These are similar to demand curves "but are derived by keeping real incomes constant and finding the marginal price for the quantity of the public good that will keep total utility unchanged". Use of such curves leads to the efficiency condition Σ marginal rates of substitution = marginal cost.

16 Quoted in W.J. Baumol (1965)
17 M. Olson Jr. (1971) p.47
18 J.M. Buchanan (1968) p.89
19 See M. Bacharach (1976)
20 The reader will find a review of such decision making rules in W.J. Baumol (1977). He is encouraged to test them against the alternatives to confirm how reliable is the prediction that the individual will not contribute. Note that the approach of weighting both equally when you are uncertain conforms to Bayes criterion.
21 See for example, A.J. Culyer (1971)

22 M. Olson Jr. (1971) p.64

23 David B Johnson (1973) refers to the work of the German
    philosopher, Immanuel Kant, who argued that "goodness"
    required complete separation from personal gain of
    the individual decision-maker. One can then
    distinguish the act of contributing (Kantian motive)
    from the benefits to be obtained from accomplishing the
    act.

    An explanation for charitable activity in this respect,
    emphasises the "private" benefits from such action.
    Similarly there may be prestige and social recognition
    implied by the "act".

    The issue does touch generally on the appropriateness
    of applying the 'economic' behaviour of individuals in
    the market to decision-taking of a 'political' nature.
    In the latter environment they may be more readily
    aware of the effects their decision have on others.
    Colm (1956), has argued that they may have an ordering
    of social wants which take precedence over private
    wants and that are pertinent in such 'political'
    situations. The 'free-rider' problem exists however
    to the extent that it is the end result that is pursued.
    J.S. Coleman (1966) follows an idea put forward by
    Adam Smith (The Theory of Moral Sentiments, London
    1825). He argues that in the same way that a firm
    invests in another firm, investment of a psychic
    nature is made by each individual in other individuals,
    groups or organisations. e.g. an individual supports
    a football team and "gains" as the team is successful.
    In such a way a 'private' return can be thought
    possible when an individual is a member of an
    association, even though his contribution does not
    add to that success. Membership of the association or
    indeed of a nation brings its own gain. To the
    extent that membership is undertaken to affect the end
    result this is not however relevant.

24 M. Olson Jr. (1971) makes this distinction (e.g.
    p.36-43) and it is one that can be applied to explain
    the early formation of the Association.

25 Ibid, p.34

5 The British Medical Association and the closed shop

The conclusions following the effect of large numbers on the provision of collective goods may be reconciled with the fact that doctors join the BMA, if membership of the BMA were compulsory. The choice of contribution towards a collective good is then taken out of the hands of the individual. Some professional associations have adopted the status of a pre-entry closed shop e.g. as far as barristers are concerned no one who is not a member of one of the four Inns of Court, is allowed to plead a case before any one of the higher courts, while for veterinary surgeons, membership of the Royal College of Veterinary Surgeons is a condition of employment. (1) The BMA however has always resisted the adoption of either official pre-entry or post-entry closed shop status. The attitude of the BMA towards a closed shop was made clear in the 1940s. In 1946, with the repeal of the Trades Disputes and Trades Union Act of 1927, it became lawful for local or other public authorities to make as a condition of employment that members of its staff should belong to unions or other such associations. The BMA responded to this by issuing a letter to all local authorities dated 16 December, 1946. In this it stipulated that, "The Association prefers that its membership should be voluntary..." and that it was "opposed on principle to a practitioner being required to join any body, British Medical Association or other..." (2)

During the history of the BMA there has always been a significant proportion of the medical profession who have practised without subscribing to the Association. (3) However, the absence of a formal closed shop does not preclude the possibility that at various times certain sections of the profession have not been subjected to informal pressures which may intimidate them into membership. In such a respect the American Medical Association proves an example par excellence. Whilst assuming a 'voluntary' status it nevertheless has possessed a network of influence which might 'persuade' practising physicians in particular to seek membership. A review of this network appears a useful prelude to an investigation of the BMA.

The AMA has attained a membership of approximately 75 per cent of American MDs. (4) However, of those physicians engaged in private practice about 90 per cent sought membership. (5) A 1960 study indicated that only 35 per cent of the physicians not in private practice, e.g. in the armed services, medical schools, etc. were AMA members. The difference appears significant, and leads one to question whether or not the practising physician falls more easily under the powers of the AMA.

The powers of the AMA originated with the Flexner Report

of 1910. Abraham Flexner, representing the Carnegie Foundation, inspected American medical schools and his report, which was critical of many schools, persuaded legislators that only graduates of first class medical schools should be permitted to practise medicine. The authority to determine a first class medical school fell to the Council on Medical Education and Hospitals of the AMA. Should a school fail to meet the standards stipulated by the Council, then loss of approval by the Council, would make it extremely difficult for that school's graduates to obtain licenses. Friedman (1962) has therefore argued that by directly exerting pressure on schools to restrict admissions, or by requiring high quality standards the AMA can restrict the supply of physicians. This of course would earn existing physicians an economic rent, which has been estimated to be as high as 20 per cent of their income. (7)

Yet the licensing powers of the AMA have proved of wider value. Part of nearly every American doctor's medical education has consisted of hospital service known as residency. Such training has been administered by hospitals, and in order to undertake it the hospitals have had to obtain the approval of the AMA. Each approved hospital has been allocated a quota of positions that can be filled by interns as part of their training. This quota has been highly prized by the hospitals as it is possible to produce medical care more cheaply with interns than without. If a hospital lost its class A rating then the loss of interns implies higher costs of production and a deterioration in the competitive position of that hospital vis-a-vis other hospitals in the medical care market. Not surprisingly, therefore, hospitals may respond to "suggestions" of the AMA to compose their staff solely of members of local medical societies. Each practising physician has been dependent on the use of hospital facilities in order to compete with his rivals. To that extent being cut off from local society membership and from hospital facilities would amount to a partial revocation of the license to practise medicine. (8)

The influence of the AMA has therefore been considerable and easily explains its high membership. Membership of the Association has proved important in many cases in order that a doctor attain admission to speciality board examinations, success in which is a necessary condition for speciality ratings. (9)   Also, of course, officials of the AMA were to be found on the very bodies that issue licenses. In the USA fifty five legally constituted medical examining boards were granted authority to issue licenses to practise medicine and surgery. It is claimed that the policies of the various state bodies of medical examiners were virtually identical with those of the AMA. (10)   This is an inevitable product of the fact that in about half the states the medical society has recommended appointees to the state board, in others the society has nominated candidates for the office, and in one case the State Medical Society Board of Censors itself has constituted the State Board of Medical Examiners.

The AMA then without question has controlled a web of influence which may effectively intimidate practising physicians at least into membership of the Association. (11) When officially it has not enjoyed the status of a closed shop, informally it has attained the same ends. The questions therefore to be asked of the BMA are twofold. Firstly, in what way does the BMA pursue goals for which an official closed shop may be valued? Secondly, to what extent does this intimidate doctors to join the BMA?

The objectives which are attainable with closed shop status may be classified as: restriction of the supply of labour; reduction of inter-union rivalry; discipline of members, particularly during strike action. (12) However there is also the possibility that benefits reaped in these areas may be achieved at the loss of sympathy from the public and within the profession if official closed shop status be declared. Depending on the efficiency of the BMA in attaining these objectives, the loss of sympathy in assuming closed shop status may well be a real cost and may help explain the association's continued rejection of overt closed shop status. With this view in mind one can survey the history of the BMA to show that it has functioned as well, if not better, without the formal and official use of a closed shop. (13)

Any association may well court the disfavour of the general public by relying on the use of closed shop power. A Gallup Poll on the Trade Unions in 1959 found that 55 per cent of the working population thought that members of trade unions are not justified to put pressure on non-members to join the union, even if this improved their negotiating power. (14) This public disfavour may be of particular importance to the BMA. In the first instance, the BMA directly negotiates with representatives of the general public and hence may prize the approval and sympathy of the general public even more highly. Secondly, experience has shown that the provision of goods and services of a medical nature can engender quite an emotive public interest, and it may well, therefore, be more important that the BMA appears to have limited coercive influence over individual doctors. For both these reasons, the BMA may present itself more easily as 'the voice of medical opinion', if it is not a closed shop. Further to this the BMA might also suffer by use of a closed shop in so far as this brought into the Association recalcitrant members. Certainly there is evidence that doctors may not wholeheartedly approve of closed shop procedure. The incident in 1946 led to many irate letters in the columns of the British Medical Journal at the prospect of a closed shop. (15) If officials within the BMA are interested in a "quiet life" they may then be reluctant to take any steps towards a closed shop. It is not surprising in this sense that McCarthy found within trade unions that the concept of closed shop was more agreeable to the militant rank and file rather than to the leadership. (16)

There would therefore be costs to the BMA in assuming official closed shop authority, while alternative means have existed to attain the ends of a closed shop arrangement.

5.1   RESTRICTION OF THE SUPPLY OF DOCTORS

One of the potential 'benefits' of closed shop activity is the possibility of restricting the supply of labour. If, before being able to take up employment, an individual must be accepted by the association, then the association has a method of restricting the labour supply and possibly of influencing its remuneration. The closed shop in this way has been of particular importance to unions where the supply of labour is seasonal and non-specific, e.g. seamen's and dockers' unions. In the case of doctors, however, much has been achieved by pressure on government rather than by closed shop authority.

The mid-nineteenth century stands as an obvious example of a period when alarm about the supply of practitioners was evident. The result was that the profession petitioned Parliament. An indication of the extent of this activity was the fact that between 1840 and 1858 seventeen bills calling for some form of medical reform were presented before Parliament. (17)   The result was an act which did not prevent competition to "qualified" practitioners by quacks but which did, as Professor Lees (1966) noted, provide distinct competitive advantages to the doctor who was on the Medical Register. The quack might be fined if he referred to himself as a "doctor of medicine" or took any title which might give the impression that he was qualified. He did not have the right to recover at law any charges for his activity, nor was he able to certify to statutory documents, e.g. death certificates. Possibly most important in terms of affecting the supply of medical practitioners, was that only those with their names on the Medical Register could take up posts within government administered services. With the introduction of the National Health Insurance scheme in 1911 and the National Health Service Act of 1946, this privilege may have meant more than was envisaged in 1858. Honigsbaum (1970) commented on the situation after 1911

"What they (the profession) wanted most of all was protection against the competition of unqualified practitioners. Here .... the 1858 Medical Act and the 1911 National Insurance (NHI) Act satisfied much of their needs ..... In America by contrast the doctors ..... never received even the numerical security granted in Great Britain in 1858. To this day, the only real safeguards American doctors have

against "unregulars" like "chiropractors" are their
own skills and the wonders of medical science." (18)

The 1858 Medical Act was of course followed by the 1886
Amendment Act which ensured that for entry to the Medical
Register doctors must qualify in surgery, physic, and
midwifery and not merely in any one of these. As the
General Medical Council enthusiastically raised the
standard of qualification for entry the supply of qualified
practitioners fell alarmingly. In 1866, for example, they
resolved that Greek should become a compulsory subject. By
1869, however, they were forced to accept that to insist
on this requirement at that stage would mean that there
would soon be no doctors to attend the poor. (19)   Even
so the GMC retained a strict control over entry as is
evident by their outlawing of the process of "covering"
at the turn of the century. (20)

The struggle to limit competition was to continue during
the twentieth century. Offensives were launched against
patent medicines as well as quack doctors; and the
occasional trophy was gained. For example, the Venereal
Diseases Act of 1917 prohibited practice by the unqualified
in relation to these diseases wherever the Act had been put
in force by the Ministry of Health. (21)   Also, in 1939
the BMA contrived to have a clause inserted in the Cancer
Act which forbade anyone but a registered medical
practitioner from treating, or offering to treat cancer
by advertisement or any other means. (22)   In 1941 the
Pharmacy and Medicines Act placed similar controls over
the treatment of a long list of serious diseases, e.g.
Bright's disease, cataract, diabetes, epilepsey or fits,
glaucoma, locomotor ataxy, paralysis or tuberculosis. (23)

It is probably an example of the profession's success
against quacks and patent medicines that in the later part
of the twentieth century panic arose about the growing
supply of qualified practitioners. The profession would
not be concerned for long, as a government committee,
working with incorrect estimates, would take steps to
restrict this supply. In 1951 The Lancet suggested that
the number of doctors qualifying in England and Wales was
about 200 in excess of the number of permanent posts
available. (24)   In 1953 it again drew attention to this,
(25) and by 1954 the British Medical Journal reported that
the General Medical Services Committee recommended that
the BMA invite the Ministry of Health to set up a working
party to examine the situation. It saw a great danger in
what it called the "obvious risks of overcrowding to the
profession." (26)

The Willink Committee duly investigated and in 1957
recommended a reduction of student intake by a tenth from
as early a date as practicable. (27) Interestingly,
B. Abel-Smith and K. Gales reported that the intake of
medical students had been reduced by about 10 per cent

before waiting for the recommendations of the report. (28)
As concern soon developed over the possibility of a doctor
"shortage" in the 1970s, the "problem" of too many doctors
appears to have been too harshly dealt with. (29)   Yet
even in the late 1950s when "overcrowding" of doctors had
generated great anxiety, there was no evidence of widespread substantial unemployment of doctors. (30)

It would appear fair to comment, as a result of this
history, that the medical profession is not one which needs
to be over concerned about restriction of the supply of
labour. Even so they have, of course, been openly
criticised for practising measures which could be
interpreted as supporting this end. For example, the
Monopolies Commission pointed to the requirement that
recognition of foreign medical qualifications was not based
solely on the merit of the medical qualification, but also
on whether there were reciprocal arrangements for British
qualifications. The BMA recognised the criticism though
pointed to the fact that entry to the European Economic
Community would serve to extend such arrangements. (31)

5.2   INTER-UNION RIVALRY

The elimination of inter-union rivalry is another goal which
can be accomplished by closed shop status. This however
is another area where the BMA has proved successful without
formally making membership compulsory. Although the
challenge of alternative associations has arisen it has
rarely proved particularly dangerous. That is to say that,
without question the BMA is, and has been, the body most
able to speak for the whole profession, both in negotiation
with the government and within the internal domestic
decision making of the profession. Most recently
independent associations have sprung up to speak for
sections of the profession. However the BMA has established
a position both inside and outside the profession which is
difficult to threaten.

(a)   The position of the BMA in negotiations with the
       Government

Reference has already been made to the intimate relationship
which the BMA and the Department of Health and Social
Security might be claimed to share. Even a Minister as
hostile to the profession as Aneurin Bevan conceded that
the BMA should be carefully consulted on "all points of
high principle involving regulations." (32)

Examples have already been given to show that this
partnership functions most smoothly when the informal
relationship between BMA officials and their "opposite
numbers" at the Department are allowed to flourish. The
commitment of the Department to the BMA as the sole voice

of the profession has already been witnessed. (33)   There
are, no doubt, advantages to the Department in having one
recognised body to speak for the whole profession rather
than a multitude of mutually incompatible demands from many
practitioners' associations.

Although matters of importance are settled through
informal negotiation a measure of how far the BMA cherishes
its relationship with the Department is seen in the efforts
it takes to maintain control of its formal links. (34)
For example, when the profession negotiated the introduction
of the NHS the BMA enjoyed a position of considerable
strength within the negotiating committee. (35)   Since
this time "autonomous committees", ie..the General Medical
Services Committee and Central Consultants and Specialists
Committee, have been able to negotiate the administration
of the NHS, but their freedom to do so has been dependent
on the BMA. That is, while they have been "autonomous",
this is only in the sense that: "No action be taken by
either of these committees which may prejudice the interests
of another part of the profession without full prior
consultation with the interests concerned, and that their
autonomous powers be used so as to expedite the work of the
Association." (36)

Despite the control the BMA clings to in respect to these
committees, it only accepted two representatives of the
Medical Practitioners Union on the GMSC on obtaining
assurances: "that in any dispute with the Government the
Union's support would be forthcoming from the moment the
final decision was made, even if the Union as such had an
opposite view up to that time; and that no separate
approach would be made to the Minister of Health by the
Union on any matter affecting the terms of service of
general practitioners under the National Health Service."
(37)

In more recent years the relationship with the Review
Body on Doctors' and Dentists' Remuneration has been
called into question. Associations such as the Junior
Hospital Doctors Association and the Medical Practitioners
Union have drawn attention to the advantage that the BMA
has been given in being allowed to present their case
orally to this body. (38)

As far as a threat to membership of the BMA by other
associations is concerned it has of course been noted that
the BMA's membership is some 63,000 and the membership of
each other respective association, in the 1970s reaches
only approximatley one eleventh of this figure. (39)
Furthermore about two thirds of the membership of other
associations are also members of the BMA. (40) The inter-
union rivalry in the profession does not threaten BMA
membership significantly. The case of the Royal Colleges
is a perfect example. There is no question of their
influence in negotiations during and since the introduction
of the NHS. (41)   Yet as far as membership is concerned

they are primarily qualifying associations and eighty per cent of their membership also join the BMA. Interestingly however the importance of the Royal Colleges may be confined in the future, since for tax purposes they have established the status of charities and must be careful not to undertake activity which might be construed trade union like. (42)

Whilst the formation of 'ginger groups' might from time to time provide some anxiety to the BMA, to argue that they have been critically jeopardised by inter-union rivalry would be unfounded.

(b)   The position of the BMA in the professional world

The BMA has long enjoyed considerable influence internally within the profession. Its officials have long overlapped with the membership of the General Medical Council. Even before the advent of the directly elected proportion of GMC members the BMA had at least five of their more prominent leaders on the GMC at one time. (43)   The addition of directly elected representatives gave the BMA an important opportunity to add to this number.

The successfulness of the procedure of election of BMA representatives to the GMC is perfectly exemplified in the election of 1951, but the technique involved can be witnessed in almost every preceding election. (44)   In 1951 the BMA put forward eight candidates for eight positions as direct representatives of the profession in England and Wales. As usual, these candidates were afforded the support of the BMA and were given space in the BMJ to present their views. So effective was the support of the BMA that all eight were elected, and the only candidate to fail was the one who stood without BMA nomination. It is notable that the BMA keep strict policy rules with regard to insuring that their nominees be elected, e.g. "restricting the number of nominees eventually supported on its whip card to the number of vacancies, in order to avoid the splitting of votes which would otherwise occur." (45)

The dominance which the BMA has enjoyed can be appreciated by examining an occasion when the BMA did not involve itself in the election. In the election to the GMC of 1970-71 candidates supported by the medical publications "Medical World" of the Medical Practitioners Union, and "On Call" of the Junior Hospital Doctors Association did quite well. However, the total poll within the profession was much lower than it had been in the past. (46)

There seems to be little evidence that the position of the BMA within the profession has been seriously subject to challenge. Once again the BMA's position of influence within the profession has shown itself as capable as

89

closed shop authority in offsetting the likely rise of
rival associations.

5.3   DISCIPLINE OF MEMBERS AND STRIKE ACTIVITY

Another of the functions of closed shop arrangements is to
provide a mechanism whereby members can be disciplined, such
that no member can harm the interests of the group without
fear of retaliatory action. To a large extent, for the
medical profession, this function is performed by the
General Medical Council, though the BMA has performed a
police like activity in isolating individuals and bringing
them before the GMC. If, for example, any doctor brought
before the Disciplinary Committee was to be found guilty of
the "unethical" practice of advertising, then the group's
interests might be harmed, and he would be erased from the
Register. Such "unethical" practices are attacked in that
wide spread advertising might lead to a lowering of the
general standards of medical treatment. Hence the consumer
is protected, while medical practitioners are also protected
from their trade falling into disrepute. This argument is
questionable particularly from the consumer's point of view.
Indeed consumers have expressed a desire for more
advertising of an informative kind, e.g. on the particular
specialisms or interests of general practitioners. (47)

Discipline must appear more of a problem at times of
conflict, but, even though there is not the formal pressure
of a closed shop, this does not mean that other social
pressures cannot be mustered to keep discipline. Sir John
Conybeare relates incidents that occurred during the
struggle over the introduction of the National Health
Insurance scheme. At one stage of the conflict in 1911, the
BMA circularised both members and non-members to sign a
petition undertaking not to give any service under the NHI
scheme except by permission of the BMA. Conybeare pointed
out that, as the struggle continued,

> "The British Medical Journal of June 22, 1912, warns
> members that they must not accept appointments on
> provisional insurance committees formed under the
> Act nor even accept medical appointments in the
> Sanatoria under the Act.
>
> Attempts were made to bring pressure on consultants
> and practitioners. The latter were urged to employ
> only those consultants who had not signed. Honorary
> staffs of hospitals were told to limit appointments
> as house officers and registrars to those who had
> signified their adhesion to the policy of the
> Association.....
>
> One suggestion made which indicates the strength of
> feeling among representatives, was that the General
> Medical Council should be approached with a view to

their dealing with "blacklegs" as guilty of
infamous conduct. It was also proposed that the
names of those members of honorary staffs of
hospitals who had not signed the supplementary
pledge should be circulated to secretaries of
divisions." (48)

The use of social pressure was by no means new at the time
of the introduction of the NHI Bill. At the turn of the
century the BMA had been engaged in solving the problem of
the free treatment provided in hospital wards and outpatient departments to potential paying patients of general
practitioners. One specific stand against this practice
was made at the Great Northern Central Hospital. In 1894
this hospital introduced pay wards for the treatment of
patients a little above the poorest class. However, the
medical staff agreed to give such patients free services
provided that the patient had been admitted with the written
consent of their own medical attendant. This was not enough
of a safeguard as far as general practioners and the BMA
were concerned. Clearly pressure was to be used in this
instance for Dr. Hugh Woods, a member of the Medical
Charities Committee of the BMA wrote to say that he was
"pleased to hear on all sides firm resolves to abstain from
calling into consultation any member of the staff who gives
his services gratuitously in these pay wards." (49)

Most certainly the threat of professional ostracism was a
weapon which the profession used to discipline members in
their battles with the friendly societies at the beginning
of the twentieth century. (50) In 1906 the medical staff
of the Coventry Providence Dispensary aired two grievances.
In the first case they objected to the control of the
affairs of the Dispensary by a committee of laymen rather
than medical men. Secondly, they claimed that the wages
of many of the users of the Dispensary had risen so that
they should be denied membership of the Dispensary. As the
management committee of the Dispensary refused to take
action in sympathy with these grievances the medical staff
resigned. The Dispensary sought medical assistance elsewhere and Dr. Burke moved to the area to work for the
Dispensary in 1907.

Between 1904 and 1907 the BMA had put forward model rules
which its division could if they wished, adopt. Three of
these rules F, G and Z, contained the basis of an effective
boycott mechanism. They stipulated that no member was to
hold any professional relationship with any medical
practitioner whom the division had deemed to be guilty of
conduct detrimental to the honour or interests of the
profession. If in an emergency, such professional relations
were held with the offender, these must be reported for
investigation by the ethical committee of the BMA. It
followed then that after 1908 Dr. Burke would fall victim
of the substance of these rules. He was advised by the BMA
that he was not expected to take the post at the Dispensary,
and when he continued with this action he was expelled.

The Association informed doctors in Coventry, Birmingham, Nuneaton, Tamworth, Leicester, Northampton, Nottingham, Leamington and York, which were the areas in which Dr. Burke might look for assistance. J. McCardie commented

> "I am satisfied that the notices circulated by the
> defendants in Coventry and the surrounding divisions
> were intended to and did in fact operate coercively.
> They were more than warnings. They were threats,
> and were meant to be threats. Behind these loomed
> the power of the defendant Association and the whole
> machinery of the boycott scheme. They were emphasised
> by the "black list" published every week by the
> defendants in the BMJ." (52)

Dr. Burke was joined by Dr. Holmes and Dr. Pratt. However, with the exception of one practitioner, the BMA achieved a total boycott of those doctors even though throughout the Midlands actual membership of the Association was only 50 per cent.

Strike Action

If closed shop status might have made the BMA more successful in its collective strike action then there was possibly an argument for the adoption of such an arrangement. Indeed the major negotiations between the BMA and the government, i.e. 1911-13 and 1944-48 showed that, either because of, or in fear of, doctors breaking ranks, the BMA was forced to acquiesce. However, it is also the case that in both instances the BMA could hardly be described as defeated. In fact it was probably the success they had in establishing the conditions of the NHI and NHS schemes that led doctors to desert any exceptionally militant stand. (53) It is doubtful that a closed shop would have made any difference. Doctors in 1913 did not lightly break their pledge to the BMA, but were nevertheless eager to acquire the good conditions negotiated. On December 13, 1912 a meeting was held in the Holborn Restaurant, London, of medical practitioners who were willing to serve under the Act. They formed the National Insurance Practitioners' Association and wrote to the Chancellor asking whether doctors who took services under the Act would receive the Government's support against boycott or intimidation. On the eighteenth of December, Lloyd George replied to the letter, assuring doctors on this matter and promising Government support by every means in its power. (54)

If the absence of a closed shop arrangement has handicapped the BMA, it is of course noteworthy that the BMA has alternative weapons in its armoury. The services of doctors are such that the mere threat of strike action in the form of refusing to work within a government scheme is potent in itself. In the discussions on remuneration in 1965 Marmor and Thomas explain the BMA's success in the

92

following terms:

> "What had changed was the mobilisation of professional
> opinion. The threat to strike had intervened. The
> Ministry at no time was worried about the resignation
> of 17,000 doctors, and the BMA was never confident that
> more than a third of that number would actually go out
> of the NHS. But the fear was that substantial sections
> of the country would be faced with a crisis of medical
> supply, that a government with only a bare majority
> would face a crisis of confidence." (55)

Not only, however, has the threat of strike action been
potent, but also the BMA has found the policy of seeking
arbitration has often more than fulfilled its needs. This
is perfectly exemplified in the ruling of Sir Justice
Dankwerts in March 1952, when he adjusted the Spens award
by a betterment factor of 100 per cent for 1952, and used a
percentage of 38.7 per cent for practice expenses; both
higher than the BMA's original claims. The BMA had not been
opposed to arbitration in principle, and the lesson
learned by those who were interviewed by Marmor and Thomas,
was that it is "extraordinarily expensive to have medical
payment disputes arbitrated." (56) The Review Body set up
in 1960 was accepted by the BMA and the lessons of 1952
have been repeated, e.g. in the Review Body Award of 1966.

One of the most effective instruments open to the BMA is
the use of the BMJ to black list posts which do not meet
with the Association's requirements. The use of this
weapon was perfectly exemplified in 1920. (57) In March
of that year the Worcestershire County Council submitted
for publication in the BMJ an advertisement for seven
school medical officers. It was known that a salary of
£450 per annum was proposed, and the attention of the Clerk
of the County Council was drawn to the fact that unless a
salary of £500 a year was given the advertisement could not
be published. The Journal also refused at this time to
advertise for the Council for an assistant county medical
officer and school oculist, and an "Important Notice"
was put in the advertisement pages of the Journal regarding
the Council. The Council advertised in the lay press, but
failed to find anyone suitable. By September they had
revised their salaries such that the £450 per annum
originally intended for a school oculist was £550 per annum,
rising by £15 a year to £600. The refusal of advertisements
and the black listing can then be effective. Indeed in
1968 as a result of an Important Notice in the British
Medical Journal, and also of advice given to deans of
medical schools, recruitment to the Armed Forces was
"virtually brought to a standstill." (58)

5.4 AN ASSESSMENT

It is clear that the BMA's rejection of official closed
shop status appears a sensible policy. It does have

93

alternative mechanisms to achieve the objectives for which formal closed shop is valued. However, it may be noted that although coercion over the individual doctor has been employed for purposes of discipline, it has not been prominent in the history of the BMA. Furthermore, of importance to this study is the fact that such coercion has been rendered to make individual doctors comply with the policy of the BMA rather than to take up membership of the BMA. The incident with Dr. Burke, for example, found virtually 100 per cent of the doctors in the Midlands area complying with the policy of the BMA even though only 50 per cent were actually members of the BMA.

In this way therefore it seems realistic to make the assumption that doctors are truly free to decide to consume membership of the BMA, and to look elsewhere for the explanation for their so doing. The BMA achieves the ends for which closed shop arrangements are used by its influence with the government, with medical schools, and, through the BMJ and GMC, with the profession. The fact that coercion of the individual doctor has played a minor role in its history leads authors such as Forsythe to comment:

> "There is no question, for example, of a BMA division being able to coerce an individual recalcitrant by withdrawing his hospital admission privileges as can the American Medical Association or the Canadian Medical Association. The area of operation for the BMA is, therefore, narrowly circumscribed....." (59)

While it is accepted that the individual doctor is free to adopt membership of the BMA or not, the previous discussion raises doubts on just how "narrowly circumscribed" the BMA actually is.

NOTES

1 W.E.J. McCarthy, (1964) p.77
2 BMJ (Supp), December 28, 1946, p.166. It is noteworthy that the BMA were praised for such a stand, e.g. see The Economist, December 7, 1946, p.903
3 See fig. one, Chapter Three
4 E. Rayack, (1967)
5 Ibid
6 The Modern Hospital, Vol. 103, No.1, July 1964
7 M. Friedman, (1962) and M. Friedman and S. Kuznets, (1954)
8 R.A. Kessel, (1958,1970). It is also, of course, the case that membership of the local medical society is fundamental for the American doctor to make the contacts necessary to pursue his practice. O.Garceau (1941),

> "The social life of the county society is important to some doctors. Few can wholly disregard it, simply because a doctor can ill

afford more than a few enemies, certainly not the hostility of an organised group in positions of local prominence. His reputation is a fragile thing, and his income and practice depend upon being called in consultation, though, perhaps more vitally on being able to call his colleagues in emergencies. Ostracism becomes a terrible weapon in such a business."

9   See R.A. Kessel, (1958)
10 See E. Rayack, (1967)
11 See also Hyde and Wolff, (1954). The AMA are frequently effective in putting dissidents out of business though there is always the exception. (M. Shadid, A Doctor for the People (1939) and Doctors of Today and Tomorrow (1947)).
12 W.E.J. McCarthy, (1964)
13 P.R. Jones (1974)
14 W.E.J. McCarthy, (1964), p.3.   This view on the part of the public and trade unionists themselves appears still in evidence. An opinion poll by Market and Opinion Research International, confirm that almost half of trade unionists and a 'sizeable majority' of the public oppose such coercion. See The Financial Times, Friday, January 9, 1976, p.8
15 BMJ (Supp), November 23, 1946 and BMJ (Supp) December 28, 1946.
16 W.E.J. McCarthy, (1964) p.145
17 D. Cowan, (1969) p.33
18 Frank Honigsbaum, (1970)
19 W.H. McMenemey, (1966)
20 An account of such a system was presented in Chapter Three
21 Sir A. Newsholme, (1936) p.368
22 P. Vaughan, (1959) p.105
23 P. Vaughan, (1959) p.105
24 B. Abel-Smith and K. Gales (1964) p.7
25 B. Abel-Smith and K. Gales (1964) p.7
26 BMJ, January 2, 1954, p.33
27 Committee to Consider the Future Numbers of Medical Practitioners and the Appropriate Intake of Medical Students. HMSO. 1957
28 B. Abel-Smith and K. Gales, (1964) p.9
29 See D. Paige and K. Jones, (1966)
30 See A. Lindsey, (1962)
31 This criticism of the Monopolies Commission Report (Cmnd 4463) HMSO London 1870, was replied to by the BMA in BMJ, Supp. 15 May, 1971, p.99
32 BMJ (Supp). 1945, Vol 11, p.100 quoted in H. Eckstein 1960, p.80
33 See Chapter Three, Section 4. It is worth noting that this intimate relationship has existed in wider circle circles than merely with the Department of Health and Social Security (formerly the Ministry of Health). During the First World War, for example, the BMA had a "gentleman's agreement" with the War Office that no doctor would be drafted except through the BMA. The

BMA then called up doctors, and there was no appeal from their decision except on the ground of conscientious objection. As such the BMA was the only body of men entrusted with a like responsibility.

During this period, in April 1917, the War Office became dissatisfied with the number of doctors called up by the BMA and issued an order calling up every doctor of military age. Pressure was brought to bear by the BMA via Morant and Verrall, the Insurance Commissioners, on Lord Derby, the War Minister. The result was the prompt withdrawal by the War Office of the order.

The incident showed three things. Firstly, the informal influence the BMA had as representatives of the doctor with government departments. Secondly, the pressure they could exert to gain their own way. Thirdly, the authority they must have represented to the individual doctor. That is, whilst ostensibly a voluntary association the individual doctor was aware of the power the association could exert over his life.

34 The above account of the incident between the BMA and the War Office is more fully documented in A. Cox (1950) pp.108-110.
The BMA often prefers to negotiate informally rather than through formal channels. For an example of how able they are to get their way in this sense see Raymond Loveridge, (1971). Loveridge shows how the Whitley Councils for the profession in the NHS failed because the BMA preferred to negotiate directly.

35 The negotiating committee consisted of 31 members, 16 of whom were directly representing the BMA. See H. Eckstein, (1960) p.101

36 Quoted in the Annual Reports of the Council of the BMA

37 British Medical Association: Annual Report of Council 1950-51, para. 11, quoted in A. Potter (1961) p.66

38 Both the JHDA and HCSA have had applications for negotiating rights with the DHSS rejected, (see Mary Ann Elston (1977), p.40)

The fact that the DHSS treats its relationship with the BMA as more important than that with any other representative body of the doctors has more recently been revealed. After a long and well publicised breakdown in negotiations between the DHSS and consultants, in which the Consultants and Specialists Association had taken a leading role, terms were agreed between the DHSS and the BMA on behalf of the consultants, at a meeting to which the representatives of the Consultants and Specialists Association had not been invited. See The Economist 26th April-2 May, 1975, p.32

39 See Chapter One. The fact that membership is so high

of course means that they must be consulted. Ray
Earwicker, (1979) examines the effectiveness of the
BMA in its relationship with the TUC on matters such
as the joint attempt to formulate a scheme for a
national maternity service. The Practitioners'
Union objected to the participation of the BMA in
that "to admit any organization which was not a trade
union and not affiliated to the TUC.... would damage
the interests of both trade unionists and the medical
profession." Even if the MPU refused to take part,
however the TUC felt that the committee would not
be "representative or authoritative unless the BMA
was associated with it."

40 See Chapter Three
41 The position of the BMA with respect to the Department
    is deeply cherished. Their influence on both
    negotiating and advisory bodies is considerable. For
    example the Central Health Services Council is a
    statutory body whose function is to give advice to
    the Secretary of State on any matter which he refers
    to, and also on any matter which the Council itself
    decides to consider, within the broad framework of
    actual or possible services under the NHS. The
    Council presents its own report to Parliament and the
    Secretary of State has to supply a preface giving
    reasons if he has rejected any of its advice. Its
    composition is laid down in great detail. R.G.S.
    Brown comments, "A majority of the members must be
    medical, including the main office bearers of the
    British Medical Association and the three specialist
    Royal Colleges ex officio and others chosen after
    consultation with various medical bodies. This
    means in practice that they are chosen from names
    suggested by the BMA and the Colleges,...." See
    R.G.S. Brown, (1975), p.61
42 BMJ (September 16, 1950, pp.685-686, BMJ, March 10,
    1951, pp.533-554, BMJ, May 3, 1952, p.979
43 P. Vaughan, (1957) p.50
44 See BMJ (Supp). February 17, 1951, p.49 and BMJ (Supp)
    May 12, 1951, p.200. Also P. Ferris (1967) p.99
    who comments, "... the remaining eleven (i.e. members
    of the GMC) are theoretically chosen to represent
    the profession at large; the British Medical
    Association organizes a postal ballot and more or
    less ensures that the eleven doctors of its choice
    are elected."
45 BMA Annual Report of Council 1957-8, Appendix V,
    quoted in A. Potter, (1961) p.94
46 BMJ, May 8, 1971. p.291
47 The Consumer and the Health Service, Office of Health
    Economics, London, 1968, p.9
48 Sir John Conybeare, "The Crisis of 1911-13", The Lancet
    May 18, 1957, p.1033
49 BMJ, November 24, 1894, p.1201, quoted in Brian Abel-
    Smith, The Hospitals, 1800-1948, Heinemann, London
    1964

50   BMJ (Supp) May 4, 1946, p.711, looks back at an article
     in the Derbyshire Times, October 4, 1902. This
     discussed the fight of the profession with the
     Oddfellows and the Druids in the same terms, and the
     doctors, while willing to tend the wage-earner whose
     employment had ceased during his illness, were not
     prepared to extend this to his family while the
     breadwinner was in receipt of full wages. The Druids
     objected to paying the doctor 4 shillings at
     Chesterfield when their fellow members at Sheffield
     paid only 2 shillings and 6 pence. The Lancet at this
     time predicted professional ostracism for any medical
     man who accepted an appointment as medical officer to
     these benefit societies.
51   An account of this is available in Pratt v British
     Medical Association, (19.9), 1K.B., 244
52   Ibid, p.252
53   In 1913 the Westminster Gazette commented,

     "We all admire people who don't know when they
     are beaten. The trouble with the BMA is that it
     doesn't know when it has won"
     Quoted in E.M. Little, History of the British Medical
     Association, 1832-1932, op.cit., p.330
54   J.L. Brand, (1965) p.228
55   T.R. Marmor and D. Thomas (1972) p.432
56   Ibid, p.424
57   This example is presented in the BMJ (1920). Vol.11
     Supp., p.81, and quoted in A. Carr Saunders and
     P. Wilson, (1933) p.98
58   Dr. Derek Stevenson, Secretary of the BMA, BMJ
     Supplement 23 November 1968, p.39. This is a classic
     example of history repeating itself. About one
     hundred years prior to this incident, the Army and
     Navy Gazette accused the BMA of similarly depriving
     the Army of Medical Officers; see E.M. Little, History
     of the British Medical Association, 1832-1932, London
     1932, p.152
59   G. Forsythe, (1966) p.12

6 The BMA and club benefits

An alternative explanation for the fact that large numbers
of doctors voluntarily join the BMA may lie in the
'selective incentives' which are offered by the Association.
(1)   Selective incentives may be defined as goods and
services which bear the characteristic of being price
exclusive. That is to say receipt of such goods is
dependent upon becoming a member of the association. Such
goods need not be pure private goods in the sense of being
exclusive and rival. Indeed many such goods may be non-
rival within capacity limits. The BMA, for example,
provides a whole range of goods and services over and above
the pure public good of wage and working conditions
improvement. Membership of the BMA brings such advantages
as: a free and regular copy of the BMJ; the right to attend
local and national meetings which provide medical research,
political, and social interest; availability to advisory
assistance from local officials or from central committees
established for that specific purpose; and also the
possibility of concessions in the purchase of insurance.(2)
Whilst some of these goods may be classed as private, e.g.
the possession of a personal copy of the BMJ, others may
not be viewed as completely rival. Consumption of a local
branch meeting for example may well be non-rival within
capacity limits. Nevertheless all the services do share
the characteristic of being excludable. Hence it can be
argued that it is for these goods and services that doctors
join the BMA, and that the pure collective good it provides
is simply a 'by-product'. (3)

If the selective incentives provided by the BMA were
all purely private goods then this explanation would
immediately run into difficulties. If it was solely private
goods that doctors wanted from the BMA why then would an
association be required? Why is it that these private goods
could not be distributed through the market like any other
private goods? The fact, however, that many of the goods
the Association provides are 'impure collective goods', in
the sense of being excludable but to some extent non-rival,
maintains the raison d'etre for the BMA and indeed shows
why membership of the BMA may be large.

Goods which are excludable but non-rival to a certain
degree, are those goods and services normally provided by
clubs. (4) Sports clubs may provide such goods, e.g.
swimming pools, or social clubs may provide theatrical
entertainment. Consumption of a swimming pool or theatre
is non-rival up to capacity limits when congestion would
reduce the benefit each person received. In the case of
the BMA many historians argue that its early days were
almost completely those of a medical research club. That
is to say that the BMA provided meetings for the purpose of

listening to lectures or exchanging research or social interests. The optimal size of such a meeting may be illustrated as in the following diagram. The curve C, shows the declining cost to any member as more individuals share the costs of providing the meeting. The share of these costs is taken for simplicity to be equal amongst participants, as is the share of benefits. The B_1 curve denotes the benefits to this person as more individuals attend the meeting. Clearly this may increase at first, e.g. possibly due to the rising standards of debate as more views are aired. However, eventually the benefits per person will fall as congestion occurs. The optimal number for such a meeting would then be S_1.

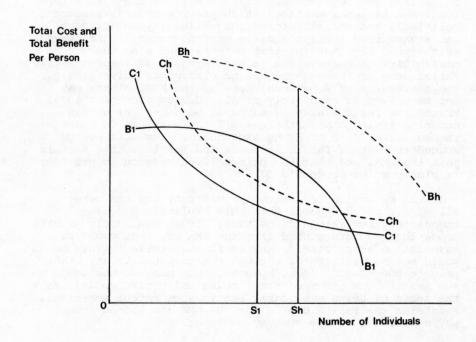

Figure 6.1 Optimal Number of Members of Clubs

100

Although this is the optimal size of the meeting it need
not of course be the optimal size of the club. The problem
of congestion is postponed by increasing the output of the
club. More than one meeting may be held. Costs for the
individual person may not rise as fast as benefits because
of the non-rivalness in consumption. Indeed there may then
be an argument for quite a large club, holding many meetings.
If h meetings were held the benefits to members of the club
may be increased by the growth of club membership to S_h.

Following this line of argument, not only does the
excludable good provide the motive for assuming membership
of the BMA, but the optimal size of the club itself, i.e.
where net benefit per person is maximised, could be large.
The precise size of the club would depend jointly on the
degree of non-rivalness in consumption of the output of the
club and the potential availability of economies to scale
in its production.

The optimal quantity of the good to be supplied is
examined in Figure 6.2. If the size of the club were j
members then no amount of the good should be supplied.
However when membership of the club reaches K then QK
meetings should be held.

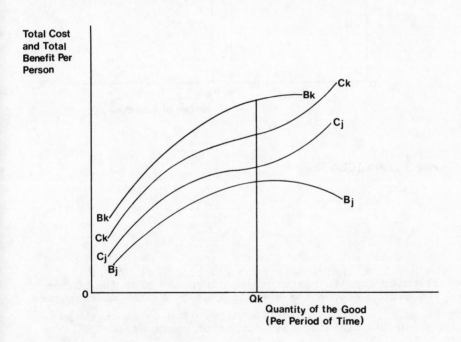

Figure 6.2 Optimal Output of Clubs

101

The following diagram shows how the establishment and growth of the BMA in a locality might be explained. From Figure 6.1 we may draw N opt which gives the value for optimal club membership for each goods quantity, and from Figure 6.2 Q opt which plots the values for optimal goods quantity for each club membership size.

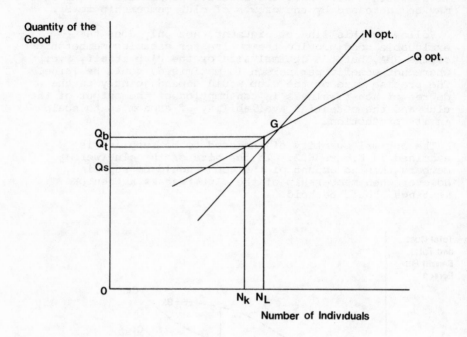

Figure 6.3 Optimal Club Size

The position indicated by G would be a position of equilibrium for the number of meetings and also the number of the club. Assume for example that Q_s branch meetings are to be held in a particular locality. The total optimal number in the club for this number of meetings is N_k. However, with N_k in the club even higher net benefit per person can be attained by the provision of Q_t meetings. With Q_t meetings N_L is the optimum club size, but such a club size calls for Q_b branch meetings in that locality. So the process continues until the equilibrium position of G is reached.

In this way therefore the club members may benefit as the club grows. The BMA metropolitan branch have in just such a manner postponed the problem of rivalness by increasing the number of divisional branch meetings in their area. In such a way therefore there is nothing to indicate that clubs must be small. If the problem of rivalness can be so postponed and if there are economies of scale, e.g. in the administration of the club as the number of meetings increase, there is no reason that club size will not grow.(5)

The argument is summarised below. The diagram shows the net benefit per person as the number of meetings increase. If only one meeting were held the club size would be small, i.e. N_1. However provision of more meetings postpones the problem of rivalness. As potential membership exceeds N_A it is feasible to establish two divisions in the area and run two meetings for membership. In the diagram optimum size for membership is N_3.

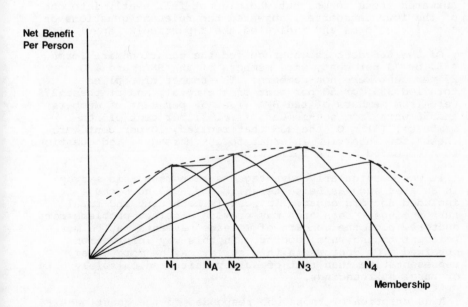

Figure 6.4 Growth of Club Membership

Enough has been said to argue the case that firstly, if
the good provided by the association is exclusive then
doctors will join in order to establish property rights to
the good, and secondly, even if the good is only non-rival
for small numbers the problem of rivalness can be postponed
by increasing the quantity of the good. On the basis of
this argument one should not be surprised that doctors join
the BMA and also that the BMA has a large membership. The
question that is begged, however, is how important are the
exclusive goods provided by the BMA to its membership. (6)
Do these exclusive goods provide the motive for membership
by comparison with the non-exclusive goods and services
the association provides?

6.1   THE IMPORTANCE OF 'SELECTIVE INCENTIVES' TO BMA
      MEMBERSHIP.

In an endeavour to provide data on the importance of 'club
benefits' to members of the BMA and to determine whether
membership depended on selective incentives, a questionnaire
sur·ey of doctors in the Leicestershire and Rutland area
was undertaken in June 1972. (7)   Four questionnaire forms
were distributed to each of the 665 doctors in the area. (8)
The forms were designed for hospital doctors and general
practitioners, both members and non-members. Each doctor
was asked to complete the relevant form. Doctors who
answered these forms, but who did not fall neatly into one
of the four categories, answered the relevant questions on
one of the forms and indicated their particular speciality.

Of the 665 doctors who received the questionnaire forms
485, or 73 per cent, were members of the BMA and 180, or
27 per cent were non-members. The number of replies
totalled 335, or 50 per cent of the total, and of these 279
were from members of the BMA (i.e. 58 per cent of members)
and 56 were from non-members (i.e. 31 per cent of non-
members). (9)   Of the 335 that replied, 10 per cent were
chosen for interview in order to ask more detailed questions
than appeared on the form. (10)

It was particularly advantageous to pursue this survey
in an area such as Leicestershire and Rutland because it
included doctors engaged in work in both city and rural
surroundings. Each area may provide distinct problems for
doctors, e.g. the concern of mileage payments may be more
relevant to the rural doctor. In this way information
obtained from doctors in this survey may be more widely
representative than that of surveys situated on solely city
or rural surroundings.

A description of those who responded to the questionnaire
survey is provided in Tables 6.1 and 6.2. Some information
is clearly shed on the work environment of members and non-
members. It appears tempting to break down the sample of
member doctors into various categories of work environment,
and compare these proportions with a similar breakdown for

non-members. This of course would have a weakness to the
extent that biases might occur in the sample, e.g. a
greater response by single handed general practitioner
members. The greater the response rate the less likelihood
there would have been of such a bias. However, since non-
members' response was not particularly strong, either in
absolute numbers, or in terms of all non-members in the area
a detailed comparison would hardly be justified. The survey
can provide no more than a tentative indicator in this
respect. It appeared for example that general practitioner
non-members and members favoured work in partnerships of
two, three and four doctors. They spend part of their time
in work in hospitals and they have endured similar periods
of hospital experience before entering general practice.
There was no indication that the extent of private practice
engaged in by doctors was greater for members than for non-
members. One could not say therefore that the growth of
partnerships of GPs or the use of hospitals, or the extent
of private practice had a noticeable effect on BMA
membership. (11)

Table 6.1
Analysis of the Response to the Questionnaire

| | Total Replies | | Members of the BMA | |
	No	Percentage of total replies	No	Percentage of total replies
General Practitioners	201	60.00	180	64.52
Hospital Doctors	118	35.22	85	40.47
Miscellaneous				
Doctors in the Armed Forces	5		5	
Doctors in Infant Clinic Work	1		1	
Doctors in Education Dept. Employment	1	16 4.78	1	14 5.01
Public Health Doctors	6		4	
Industrial Doctors	3		3	
Total	335	100.00	279	100.00

Table 6.2
Analysis of Replies from General Practitioners

	General Practitioner Total replies		General Practitioner Members of the BMA	
	No	Percentage of General Practitioners	No	Percentage of General Practitioners
Retired General Practitioners	17	8.46	16	8.89
Single handed General Practitioners	19	9.45	19	10.56
Assistant General Practitioners	7	3.48	7	3.89
General Practitioners in partnership	158	78.61	138	76.67
Total	201	100.00	180	100.00

One interesting piece of information which was unearthed by the survey was the fact that doctors tended to join the BMA promptly on attaining their first medical qualification and seldom leave the Association.

Table 6.3
The Speed with which Doctors join the BMA

	No	Per cent
Those who joined in the year of qualification	170	60.93
Those who joined one year later	37	13.26
Those who joined in the 2nd to 6th year after qualification	53	15.43
Those who joined in the 6th to 10th year after qualification	11	3.95
Those who joined in the 10th to 17th year after qualification	5	1.44
Those who joined before qualification	10	3.58
Those who did not answer the question	3	1.08
	289	100.00

The explanation for the almost automatic entrance to the BMA may be a number of factors. Firstly, the BMA has been' in existence since 1832 and it may almost be described as traditional to acquire membership. Secondly, the graduation in the fees for membership of the BMA discriminates in favour of those who join early after

qualification. (12)   Thirdly, an important factor in the
formative years of a doctor's career is access to the
columns of advertisements of vacant positions in hospitals
and general practice that are published in the BMJ. This
of course is available weekly to the doctor at a much
reduced rate provided that he is a member of the BMA. The
Lancet also carries such advertisements, particularly of
hospital posts; and literature circulated by drug
manufacturers is beginning to provide such information.
However, doctors interviewed in the sample stressed the
importance of the wider scope of advertisements presented
in the BMJ. Also some indicated the ease of availability
of the BMJ by membership of the BMA, rather than, for
example, competing for it in hospital libraries. Although
the Professional and Executive Register of the Department
of Employment placed a small number of doctors and although
word of mouth was a useful source of information of
vacancies, the BMJ appeared particularly useful in this
respect. It would appear that its pre-eminence depends upon
the scope of advertisements, and the advantages of acquiring
a personal copy helped explain the early membership of the
BMA by doctors.

However, while the individual doctor is quick to join the
BMA he is slow, even after settling in an appointment, to
leave. In the survey 82.80 per cent of members of the BMA
had never left. This finding would seem to suggest that
there are many other individual services that are of
importance to the doctor. It is then to an examination of
the exclusive goods and services provided by the BMA that
attention is focused. The survey attempts to answer the
question of their importance to the average individual
doctor.

(a) Local services

The regular branch meetings provided by the BMA may be
thought of as important to doctors for the interchange of
scientific, medical and political ideas. Surprisingly,
however, doctors in the Leicestershire and Rutland area
take little interest in such meetings. In fact, however,
almost two thirds of members had not attended one.

Table 6.4
Attendance of local branch meetings
between January 1970 and June 1972.

Members attending one or more meetings	35.1 per cent
Members attending no meetings	62.4 per cent
Those who did not answer this question	2.5 per cent
	100.0

It was the case also, for those who attended meetings, that the larger proportion were not regular in attendance. Clearly two thirds of those that did attend never attended more than twice.

Table 6.5
Frequency of attendance of local branch meetings between January 1970 and June 1972

Members attending once only   32.6 per cent
Members attending twice only   28.6 per cent
Members attending three times or more 38.8 per cent

                                      100.0

The percentage of those attending local branch meetings differed little between hospital doctors and general practitioners. In the case of hospital doctors 35 per cent attended, but of these 67 per cent attended no more than twice. Similarly 36 per cent of general practitioners attended and of these 61 per cent attended no more than twice. Forty per cent of those hospital doctors who attended, attended no more than once, and in the case of general practitioners, 31 per cent of those attending only attended once.

This lack of attendance is typical of conditions throughout the country. Dr. Roberts has presented statistics to show that, whatever the size of a division, only between ten and thirty doctors attended. (13) Indeed it would appear that the largest proportion of members attending branch meetings are those who hold office. "Enough non executive members to defeat an executive committee resolution attended in only 25 per cent of divisions. 'In other words', said Dr. Roberts, '75 per cent of division business meetings cannot vote down anything put up by the executive committee'." (14) Mr. John Pringle, Public Relations Officer for the BMA has noted the likely apathy of members of voluntary bodies, and the likelihood that only 10 per cent of members can be expected to attend meetings. (15)

However, one would expect attendance to vary with the political climate, (16) that is when the BMA is locked in controversy with the Department of Health one would expect members' interest and support to be keener. This it is, but even in the BMA's greatest controversies attendance at meetings does not seem a necessity for members. "Even at the height of the controversy leading up to the acceptance by the medical profession of the National Health Service Act in 1948, it was the exception for more than half the members of a Division of the British Medical Association to attend meetings." (17)

Evidence would suggest then that the infrequent attendance of members in the Leicestershire and Rutland area is typical of a nationwide problem with which the BMA is faced. However, in addition to branch meetings the BMA also provides purely social events. In the questionnaire doctors were asked merely had they ever attended social meetings. The question with reference to social meetings was therefore left much more open. The results show that almost half of all members make no use at all of BMA social meetings. In the case of general practitioners 44 per cent never attend and in the case of hospital doctors, 56 per cent make no use of social functions. For members as a whole 49 per cent don't attend social meetings. Furthermore, in the interviews carried out it was clear that attendance of social functions was a rare pleasure. Indeed it would appear that once in every three years would be a fair average rate of attendance. The reason often expressed for non-attendance was pressure of work.

The local services then which might be thought of as exclusive to members were not felt important by the membership. The national activity of the BMA, i.e. the political lobbying and negotiating for improvement of remuneration and work conditions, was by comparison felt to be the more important activity of the BMA.

Table 6.6
Members' preferences for
national or local activity

	Per cent of total members	Per cent of general practitioner members	Per cent of hospital doctor members
Members feeling the national activity was the more important to them.	85	83.4	89.4
Members feeling the local activity was the more important to them.	3	3.3	3.5
Members feeling they were equally important.	4	5.0	2.4
Members feeling that neither was important.	1	1.1	-
Members not answering the question.	7	7.2	4.7
	100.0	100.0	100.0

(b) Library services

In conjunction with the local services of the BMA the member can also enjoy the library services provided. The Nuffield Library at BMA House will supply either books or photocopies at a much cheaper cost to members. However, it is hardly the case that this is an important service for members in the Leicester or Rutland area. It is arguable that it is more important for hospital doctors than general practitioners, although not a large proportion of hospital doctors use this facility.

Table 6.7
Members' use of Library facilities

	Per cent of total of members	Per cent of general practitioners	Per cent of hospital doctors
Members using library services.	17.2	14.4	22.4
Members not using library services.	80.6	82.8	76.5
Members not answering this question.	2.2	2.8	1.1
	100.0	100.0	100.0

Furthermore, of those members that used the library services during the period, 27 per cent used it once only and 10 per cent used it twice only.

The figures that emerge from this survey in respect of the use of library facilities seem to concur with those experienced throughout the country. "Figures for the past ten years indicate that between 10 per cent and 20 per cent of the total membership make use of the library annually." (18)

(c)   Insurance concessions

The library facilities then appear of little significance to the average member, as do the insurance concessions offered by the BMA. Such concessions are represented by the BMA, Personal Accident Insurance Schemes which provides a wide cover and under which a BMA member who takes out £10,000 of insurance is told he will save £1.25 per annum. (19)
Also there are certain concessions which BMA members can claim with the Medical Insurance Agency. The results of the survey show, however, that the large majority of BMA membership in the Leicestershire and Rutland area did not take advantage of any such concessions. Again there was little difference in the results as between hospital doctor and general practitioner.

Table 6.8
Members' use of insurance concessions

	Per cent of total members	Per cent of general practitioners	Per cent of hospital doctors
Members taking advantage of insurance concessions.	34.8	36.7	34.1
Members not taking advantage of insurance concessions .	64.5	62.8	64.7
Members not answering the question.	0.7	0.5	1.2
	100.0	100.0	100.0

(d)   Advisory services

An allegedly important service provided by the BMA is the advice which it can provide for doctors. "As motorists use the Automobile Association for advice about fog and traffic jams, so doctors use the BMA for advice on partnership agreements, ethics, pensions and expenses." (20)

Advisory services appear of importance to doctors particularly as the increasing regulations of the National Health Service make life more complicated. The BMA has three standing Advisory Bureaux. Firstly, there is the Commonwealth and International Medical Advisory Bureau which has as its main activity that of advising overseas doctors on matters such as registration, training and employment in this country. Use of this body has increased from approximately 700 inquiries per year in 1948 to 3,200 inquiries in 1968. (21) Secondly, there is the Medical Practices Advisory Bureau which has played an important role in finding appointments for doctors. This has become all the more important for general practitioners with the complications created by the Medical Practices Committee in regulating the movement of doctors in the country. The Medical Practices Advisory Bureau also acts as a locum agency, providing temporary appointments. Together with the Medical Practices Advisory Bureau there stands the final advisory body, i.e. the British Medical Association Career Service. This third body deals with such problems as entry into medical schools, financial support for mature students, pre-registration posts for doctors.

The extent of the influence of all three bodies is not that extensive. In 1971 there were 829 total inquiries for the BMA Career Service. (22) There were 1,935 written enquiries and 3,906 personal visits of inquiries to the Commonwealth and International Bureau. The Medical

Practices Advisory Bureau dealt with 106 partnership vacancies; 193 requests for copies of forms on agreements between principals and assistants; 1,159 principals in general practice who requested help in finding a locum (664 of whom were actually helped); 5,598 requests for locums which appeared from hospitals (697 of which were filled). Even assuming that all these inquiries for advice and help represent inquiries from different members of the BMA this only represents 19.6 per cent of the total membership of that year.

Clearly this percentage may be an under estimate to the extent that doctors can get advice from local officials rather than by recourse to bureaux at headquarters. The results of the survey at Leicestershire and Rutland take this factor into account by asking a general question as to whether or not recourse had been made to the BMA for advice. It appeared that the majority of members had at some time sought advice from the BMA. This was more especially the case with general practitioner members than hospital doctor members.

Table 6.9
Percentage of members' using advisory services

	Per cent of total members	Per cent of general practitioner members	Per cent of hospital doctor members
Members using advisory services of the BMA.	58.4	72.2	32.9
Members not using advisory services of the BMA.	41.6	27.8	67.1
	100.0	100.0	100.0

Although a majority of members had turned at some time or other for advice from the BMA, it appeared clear that almost half of those who did ask for advice, were seeking help with only one sort of problem, e.g. ethical procedure, taxation problems, contract difficulties.

Table 6.10
Percentage of members' using advisory services for one or more problems

	Per cent of members	Per cent of general practitioner members	Per cent of hospital doctor members
Members seeking advice on one area of difficulty	44.8	40.8	67.9
Members seeking advice in two areas	30.7	22.8	21.4
Members seeking advice in three areas	14.1	11.1	10.7
Members seeking advice in four or more areas	10.4	25.3	-
	100.0	100.0	100.0

It was possible, from the questionnaire form, to provide an indication as to what form of problems provide doctors with the greatest difficulties. Doctors indicated which area of difficulty caused them need to resort to the BMA. The number of those ticking each particular problem on the form was taken as a percentage of the total number of doctors seeking advice. As these problems were not mutually exclusive, and as a doctor might tick more than one, there is no reason for the following percentages to sum to 100. Nevertheless, the table does provide a comparison of the relative importance of each area of difficulty.

Table 6.11
Percentage of members' using advisory services for particular problems

	Per cent of total members using BMA advice
Members seeking advice on ethics	35.0
Members seeking advice on career	12.9
Members seeking advice in practice	21.5
Members seeking advice in setting up practice	35.6
Members seeking advice in setting fees	47.2
Members seeking advice in financial matters	11.7
Members seeking advice on some other matter	30.7

113

Though, to general practitioners at least, the advisory services may be important it is difficult to argue that they are a strong incentive to join the BMA. It is noteworthy, for example, that it was only in December 1968, that the Council decided that the Bureaux should make charges for services to doctors who are not members of the Association, (23) and this had little noticeable effect in increasing membership. Returns from non-members showed they had used the BMA for advice as non-members, and in interviews some felt confident of being able to do this in the future without becoming members.

Before leaving the discussion of advisory services it should be noted that the BMA is not particularly active in the provision of medical defence for doctors. In America, the AMA is very active in this role, (24) but in Britain such services are performed by specialist defence associations, e.g. the Medical Defence Union and the Medical Protection Society. This is not to say that the BMA has not considered extending its influence. In 1887, 1897, 1903, and 1914 proposals to extend such services were discussed by the BMA. In 1920 the MDU and MPS were unsuccessfully approached by the BMA in the hope that they would provide concessions for BMA members if they joined en bloc. (25) The BMA, then unlike the AMA has less to offer members in this respect. To the extent that BMA assistance is of value in times of trouble the individual doctor might choose to join as he perceives trouble looming on the horizon.

THE BRITISH MEDICAL JOURNAL

In looking to the services provided by the BMA one must not neglect the provision to each member of the British Medical Journal. It has been claimed that receipt of the American Medical Journal is an important factor in accounting for membership of the AMA. "The importance of this attraction is perhaps indicated by a survey conducted in Michigan which showed that 89 per cent of the doctors received the Journal of the American Medical Association and 70 per cent read a state journal but less than 20 per cent read any other type of medical literature." (26)

In Britain there is evidence that the BMJ is similarly widely read. A survey on reading rates of medical journals was carried out on general practitioners by the Government Social Survey for the Sainsbury Committee. (27) The results of this survey are shown as follows:

Table 6.12
Proportion of general practitioners saying that they regularly looked at the specified journals and periodicals

Name of journal or periodical	Proportion of general practitioners regularly looking at each journal or periodical
British Medical Journal	84 %
The Lancet	13 %
The Practitioner	60 %
Journal of the College of GPs	26 %
Prescribers' Journal	85 %
Drug and Therapeutic Bulletin	19 %
Pulse	73 %
Modern Medicine	59 %
Medical News	49 %
Medical World News Letter	55 %
World Medicine	51 %
Medical Tribune	29 %
Medical World	44 %
Others specified	31 %

Clearly the 84 per cent of general practitioners who 'regularly looked' at the BMJ is impressive by comparison with the 13 per cent that looked at The Lancet. The problem is however, of comparing like with like. That is to say that the doctors having assumed membership of the BMA receive their copy of the BMJ 'free'. The question is therefore whether individual doctors join the BMA to read their own copy of the BMJ or whether they look regularly at the BMJ because they receive it free as a result of their membership. A comparison of BMJ reading rates with other journals or periodicals received free of charge seems to reduce the importance of the BMJ. For example 73 per cent looked regularly at Pulse while 85 per cent looked regularly at Prescribers' Journal.

A survey was carried out in 1972 of some 4,541 hospital doctors for the British Journal of Hospital Medicine. (28) The survey had a 57 per cent response rate and was followed up with personal interviews. The interesting feature was that again hospital doctors appeared to find the BMJ more useful than The Lancet. In terms of such criteria as: "keeping up with advances in medicine"; containing "useful items on my speciality"; "presenting a balanced view of medicine"; "useful for light reading" and "for book reviews", those who responded to the questionnaire rated the BMJ more highly than The Lancet. Yet the British Journal of Hospital Medicine distributed freely to NHS doctors attained an even better score than the BMJ. The BMJ appeared superior to both The Lancet and the British Journal of Hospital Medicine for "news of people and events in medicine" and particularly "for job advertisements."

There appears alternative medical literature therefore that British doctors consult as frequently as the BMJ. It would be wrong to interpret the high reading rate of the BMJ in terms of doctors depending on it. Indeed it would be misleading to base any interpretation of the respective values of the BMJ and The Lancet totally on these reading rates. While the findings of the Sainsbury Committee show reading rates higher for the BMJ, surveys of reading rates in medical libraries show a greater dependence on The Lancet. In a survey on the use of periodicals in British medical libraries, Pendrill claims that the Lancet is a more popular journal than the BMJ. W. Mell argues that, while the Lancet is essential for small hospital libraries, the BMJ may be considered as a supplementary periodical. Furthermore L.M. Raising in reviewing world biomedical journals between 1957-60 would attach greater importance and significance to The Lancet than to the BMJ. (29)

The overriding importance of the BMJ in terms of reading rates should not be interpreted as an explanation for membership of the BMA. That is, reading of the BMJ may be a result of the receipt of a free copy rather than because of the essential nature of the contents. In interviews with doctors in the Leicestershire and Rutland area reading of the BMJ referred in the main to scanning the contents and very rarely ever returning to actually read a particular article. Butler and Stokes found similar difficulty in relying on the answers to the rather ambiguous term "reading". They note that "a remarkably large proportion of trade unionists, 65 per cent, claim to read these (union) journals and two thirds of these claim to pay "some" or a "good deal" of attention to them. However, since these journals give substantial coverage to policies, especially at election time, it is startling to find that only 30 per cent of their readers, that is to say only 20 per cent of all union members, could recall after the 1946 election having seen any articles on political questions". (30)

In the Leicestershire and Rutland survey some indication of the importance of the BMJ to the doctor was sought by assessing the need of non-members of the BMA to fill the gap of the non receipt of the BMJ by subscribing to some other journal. The results show that the non-members of the BMA had little need, in comparison with the members of the BMA, to subscribe to other medical literature. This may, of course, be due to the fact that members of the BMA are more avid in reading journals. However, evidence may suggest that it is because receipt of the BMJ is in no sense essential to the doctor.

Table 6.13
Subscription to Medical Journals

	Members	Non-members
Per cent of GPs subscribing to any other journal than the BMJ	65	57
Per cent of GPs subscribing to The Practitioner	55	38.1

The results of the survey were consistent with the results of the Sainsbury Committee in finding The Practitioner an important journal to which doctors subscribe. The Sainsbury Committee found that 60 per cent of doctors "look through most issues" of The Practitioner. They found that young doctors up to the age of 39 considered The Practitioner the best source of information of drugs. Also doctors in partnerships of three or more found The Practitioner a better source than the BMJ for information on drugs.

In a survey of the sources of information for general practitioners Wilson et al have found that the medical journals are not particularly important for the GP. They look to the source of information on prescribing by general practitioners and found medical journals an unimportant influence in comparison with information gained from representatives and postal communications from the pharmaceutical industry. (31) This is clearly shown in the following table where the sources of information for treating various illnesses are shown. The small importance of medical journals in providing information would then hardly suggest the BMJ is essential to doctors.

It is submitted then that doctors do not join the BMA primarily to maintain throughout their years of practise receipt of the BMJ. Indeed figures between 1900 and 1950 show that publication of the BMJ fluctuates directly with membership of the BMA. It is the case then that when doctors leave the BMA they do not feel it necessary to subscribe independently to the BMJ. This may suggest that this reading of the BMJ is dependent on their membership of the BMA, and not necessarily that the BMJ is so vital that they feel compelled in any sense to join the BMA.

Table 6.14

Percentage of prescribing for specific clinical conditions due to different therapeutic sources

Therapeutic Source

Clinical Condition	Medical Training	Consultant Advice	Textbooks	Periodicals Medical Journals	B.N.F.	Prescribers' Journal	M.I.M.S.	Drug Firms	Discussion with G.P. Colleagues
Tonsils to trachea	22.7	12.3	4.0	4.4	15.2	1.9	3.1	29.2	6.4
Otitis media	30.2	9.5	3.3	6.6	9.4		1.9	36.5	2.2
Nesopharynx, coryza, etc	35.6	4.0	0.6	3.1	28.2	0.1	5.3	17.7	5.4
Bronchitis	36.0	5.4	4.3	5.1	17.4	0.1	2.0	21.8	7.9
Chronic bronchitis emphysema	31.2	4.8	2.2	6.1	20.0	0.4	3.8	26.6	4.9
Heart disease	47.3	19.5	2.2	8.8	5.3	0.8	0.8	14.4	0.8
Hypertension, nephritis	22.0	17.4	9.0	9.8	15.4	0.9	3.0	22.2	1.3
Alimentary infections	31.6	7.1	2.7	4.6	15.2	0.8	14.3	19.7	3.9
Peptic ulcer, dyspepsia	38.3	6.9	2.7	6.2	22.8	0.6	2.8	18.3	2.7
Anaemia	27.3	19.2	1.1	6.8	9.3	0.8	4.7	27.9	2.9
Influenza	31.3				37.1	0.9	2.0	17.2	5.5
Skin: sepsis	35.6	5.0	2.3	12.1	8.6		4.0	29.3	2.5
Skin: other	24.4	23.8	2.9	8.8	7.1	0	2.4	27.1	3.5
Genito-urinary: male and female	33.9	16.1	3.2	6.5	16.0	1.5	3.0	18.1	1.8
Pregnancy: natal, pre, post	41.0	3.8	2.8	14.3	23.0	0.7	0.7	13.2	0.3
Rheumatism, neuralgia fibrositis	25.1	3.7	1.8	6.0	18.3	1.2	4.7	36.6	2.5
Arthritis joint injury	39.9	12.4	2.0	4.0	9.2	0.7	5.2	24.0	2.6
Neuroses, functional disease	26.0	13.8	2.0	7.9	13.4	0.1	6.2	27.4	3.1
Psychoses, schizoid depression	16.0	44.7		8.3	9.5			19.0	2.6
Injuries and sequelae	53.4	6.0	2.6	1.7	13.8	0	1.7	19.8	0.8

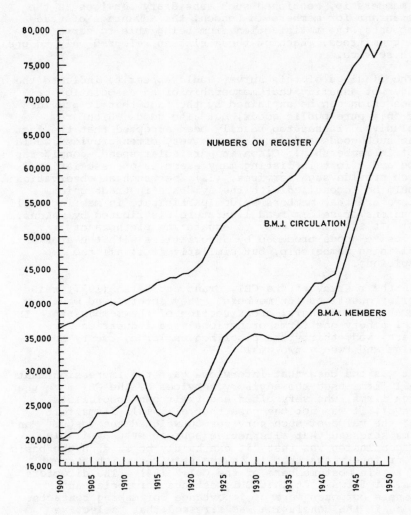

Figure 6.5 The BMJ Circulation 1900-1950

6.2   AN ASSESSMENT

The main exclusive goods and services provided by the BMA
have been outlined. They clearly do not appear in any

sense essential to its membership. A certain number of other services were mentioned, but these were clearly of even less significance. Sixteen members, or 5.7 per cent of membership, mentioned such subsidiary services as the restaurant for members in London, the advantage of trade discounts, the satisfaction from being able to serve on BMA committees. Each of these sixteen referred only to one such service.

The findings of this survey would appear to indicate the danger of assuming that membership of an association or trade union can be explained by the fact that it provides not only pure public goods, but also goods which are exclusive. It has too readily been accepted that the fact that such goods and services are very often provided would explain membership. Olson in particular spends considerable time and effort in listing many examples of associations which provide such services. (32) Yet such an observation should be reconciled with the evidence in trade union literature that members seldom participate in meetings held by unions or seldom read literature distributed by unions. (33) It is all too easy to equate the plethora of exclusive goods produced by associations with the arguments explaining membership, but similarly it is all too suspicious.

In their study of the CBI, Grant and Marsh (1977) raise similar questions for members. They interviewed what was arguably a meaningful cross section of the membership. In total ninety one firms or nationalised industries were interviewed; thirty one described as large, twenty seven medium and twenty two small.

It was the case that interviews gave the impression that small firms used the advisory services of the CBI more than large firms, who very often had their own specialists. However, it was not the case that all small firms felt that the value of such services outweighed the costs. Many firms stressed that alternative sources were available. The conclusion was that "it can hardly be said on the basis of our interviews that it is the services which attract and retain most members of the CBI." (34) The directors of small firms felt that CBI meetings for social and business purposes were of importance for making contacts. But again the conclusion was stressed that "selective incentives seem in most cases to be of marginal importance." (35)

As far as coercion is concerned the CBI has no closed shop and can impose no sanctions on firms who refuse to join. (36) It would appear then that the collective good is important and "most members seem to value the supply of the collective good at least as much as the supply of selective incentives." (37) It is the case that "the CBI does not sell itself largely on selective benefits." (38)

The argument that members only join for the exclusive goods provided by the association, is also highly questionable in the light of the fact that all associations providing such goods still produce the pure public goods which are non-exclusive. It would seem a fair assumption that some of their resources in terms of time and money must be devoted to this end. If it were the sole intention of members to pay subscriptions for the exclusive goods then why is there not a rise of associations producing only such goods? By not producing the non-exclusive goods they would be able to offer the exclusive services at a smaller subscription. (39)

Though the study of the BMA has concentrated attention on the tangible, and hence more easily quantifiable, selective incentives, enough has been said to raise doubt as to their importance. One can always construe some psychic pleasure that doctors may receive simply from the act of joining the BMA and present this as a selective incentive. The value and predictive potential of such an approach is questionable. Certainly in terms of the more tangible private goods and club benefits that are provided by the BMA enough has been said to call into question their importance in explaining voluntary membership of the Association. Note that it is not claimed that they are totally unimportant but that one should be hesitant in relying solely on these factors to explain behaviour. Olson has claimed that "An organisation that did nothing except lobby to obtain a collective good for some large group would not have a source of rewards or positive selective incentives it could offer potential members." (40) To the extent that this can be applied to an association such as the BMA, it would appear that in and of themselves this sole source of rewards does not totally explain membership and reconcile the experience of the BMA with collective good theory. A postal survey in June 1978 by the British United Provident Association (BUPA) of a random 3,000 members on BMA benefits and health insurance was carried out. It showed that 91 per cent considered the most important function of the Association to be its involvement in national negotiations on pay and conditions of service. (41)

NOTES

1   M. Olson Jr. (1965)
2   BMA advertisement handout
3   M. Olson Jr. (1965)
4   The following analysis is based heavily on J.M.Buchanan
    (1965) and Yew Kwang Ng, (1973)
5   J.M. Litvack and W.E. Oates, argue that even when
    congestion costs do occur, their cost will be offset
    to some extent by the savings which result from
    spreading the costs of output over a large number of
    consumers

6   It will be noted that the exclusive goods and services referred to with respect to the BMA are all tangible. There are probably intangible "goods" received which are also exclusive, e.g. a feeling of security, or of identity, or of integrity, which are enjoyed by the individual as a result of personal membership of the Association. Such psychological effects of membership of an association have been examined, e.g. L. Chaffen, (1947), Mark van de Vall, (1970), E Wight Bakke (1945). Here, however, attention is concentrated on the tangible exclusive benefits of membership of the BMA. Firstly, it would be difficult to test the full significance of intangible selective incentives. Secondly, there is the danger of describing too much as selective incentives and as a result losing some of the predictive bite of this argument.

7   This survey was made possible by a grant financed by the University of Leicester. It was undertaken with the kind co-operation of the British Medical Association. Dr. Derek Stevenson, the Secretary of the BMA was particularly helpful in granting me a personal interview. Dr. Parkes Bowen, the Secretary of the Leicestershire and Rutland branch, also provided considerable assistance in the formation of the questionnaire forms.

8   These questionnaire forms are shown in Appendix A of P.R. Jones, An Economic Analysis of Collective Behaviour:The Case of the BMA. (PhD. Leicester) (1976)

9   While this total is not large it is considerably larger than other sample surveys which have looked to the work of doctors, e,g. W.P.D. Logan and A.A. Cashion looked to a sample of 106 practices in Studies on Medical Population Subjects, No. 14, Vol. 1, 1958, Wilson et al looked to 39 doctors in the Liverpool area in their survey on the Influence of Different Sources of Therapeutic Information on prescribing by General Practitioners, BMJ, September 7, 1963, Vol.11, pp 599-604.

10 These 10 per cent were not chosen at random, but were chosen systematically in order to get an even distribution of doctors of all ages. Care was also taken to make this small sample representative of doctors who worked in the city of Leicester and also those who worked in more out-lying rural areas. Both general practitioners and hospital doctors were represented with the 10 per cent. Furthermore the 10 per cent was split between members and non-members in approximately the same ratio as that which applied for the total number of doctors in Leicestershire and Rutland. Although this 10 per cent sample was too small for statistical analysis it did add further insight to certain of the replies which doctors made on the questionnaire forms.

11 The data permitted a chi square test on the significance of working in general practice or hospitals on membership of the BMA. On the basis of the test it could not readily be said that such

environment had no influence. It appeared that GPs were more likely to join than hospital doctors. Eckstein, (Pressure Group Politics) argues that the BMA has always been primarily a GPs association. These results would not refute this view though the survey was taken at a time when hospital doctors felt, with some justification, that the BMA had neglected them for the GP.

The data did not support chi square tests on the other comparisons referred to in the text. The number of GP non-members replying being so small.

12 See Appendix C of P.R. Jones, An Economic Analysis of Collective Behaviour, (1976)
13 BMJ, Supp. 18 October 1969, p.16
14 Ibid, p.16
15 A. Potter (1961) p.98
16 It is noteworthy that, at such times, one would not automatically assume that, if the non-members'interest was similarly awakened, he would necessarily join the BMA. J.L. Brand (1965) points out that during the controversy over Lloyd George's National Health Insurance Bill non-members both attended and voted in BMA meetings.
17 L. Dopson (1971) p.125
18 BMJ, Supp, 26 April, 1969
19 BMA handout, 1971
20 P. Ferris (1972) p.168
21 BMJ, Supp. 26 April 1969, p.58
22 BMJ, Supp. 13 May 1972, p.107-108
23 BMJ, Supp. 26 April 1969, p.58
24 O. Garceau (1941) comments on p.103, that this is "one formal service of the society with which the doctor can scarcely dispense."
25 R. Forbes (1948)
26 M. Olson Jr. (1965) p.140
27 Report of the Committee of Enquiry into the Relationship of the Pharmaceutical Industry. Cmnd 3410 London, HMSO 1967, p.157-159
28 See P.R. Jones (1976)
29 G.R. Pendrill, Surveys on the Use of Periodicals in some British Medical Libraries, University of Sheffield Postgraduate School of Librarianship; W. Mell, "Basic Journal List for Small Hospital Libraries", Bulletin of the Medical Library Association, April 1966, Vol. 54, No.2
30 David Butler and Donald Stokes (1969) p.201
31 C.W.M. Wilson, J.A. Banks, R.E.A. Mapes and S.M.T. Korte (1963)
32 M. Olson, Jr. (1965)
33 Mark van de Vall, (1970) p.95-102, summarises a number of studies showing the poor attendance at union meetings, and p.126-127 shows that the motive for joining trade unions for personal information and advice is not important.
34 W. Grant and D. Marsh (1976) p.46

35 W. Grant and D. Marsh (1976) p.47
36 W. Grant and D. Marsh (1976) p.47, this view was
    questioned by J.R. Shackleton (1978) p.377, who would
    attach weight to the possibility of a loss of goodwill
    against non-joiners. W. Grant (1979) p.127 replies,
    "Although there were cases in our sample where such
    factors were important, I would argue that the general
    explanatory value of such pressures as a form of
    negative sanction is limited in the case of the CBI."
37 W. Grant and D. Marsh (1976) p.50
38 W. Grant and D. Marsh (1976) p.50
39 G. Stigler (1974) p.360
40 M. Olson, Jr. (1965) p.133
41 BMA Annual Report of Council 1978-79, BMJ Vol.1 p.12.
    It is noteworthy that the second most important was the
    BMJ and sixty one per cent felt that personal
    representation and advice was either fairly important
    or very important to them.

7 Leadership

The conclusion that individuals will not voluntarily subscribe to associations which produce collective goods has been arrived at with little discussion of the potential activities of the leadership of the association. Their role has implicitly been viewed as completely passive. That is to say, the association has been interpreted purely as an organisation standing by ready for individuals to approach it for membership; it has been given no other goal than the maximization of the welfare of its membership. Yet it is conceivable that the organisers of an association play a much more active role. That they attempt, for example, to entice potential contributors by altering the individual's expectation as to his efficacy in provision of the good. Furthermore, it is possible that alternative aims which reflect in part the goals of organisers can be attributed to the association. If so, how are the predictions of the likelihood of individual subscription to a non-rival, non-exclusive good altered?

It is the objective of this chapter to introduce the political entrepreneur as the individual who undertakes to mobilise collective action. Though he may pursue quite a wide range of different activities, the initial situation in which he is discussed is that where he seeks to persuade a free-rider to contribute and yet attain a reward for himself which is distinct from the collective good. To argue this case it will be clear that the individual contributor must be led to believe that his contribution is not totally meaningless and may count for something. To this end the very existence of the political entrepreneur is important. Given that the individual has little information, the appearance of an entrepreneur willing to undertake costs to canvass him for his donation must convey the impression that this donation at least counts for something. Furthermore the existence of an association with an observable membership may well give the impression that the possibility that "no one else contributes" is not so likely. The very existence of a political entrepreneur then reduces the degree of uncertainty. Yet in a more positive way he will actively persuade the individual that there may be some purpose to his contribution.

It is on this note that the second section of the chapter will begin. Though digressing slightly from the theme of the political entrepreneur per se, the objective is to consider more thoroughly the assumptions which underlie the prediction that no quantity of the collective good will be forthcoming as a result of voluntary action. In effect quite a number of assumptions are required to make the individual's action impotent; and hence the prediction of non-contribution. However, they can be relaxed slightly, even when the group is quite sizeable, so as to permit the more general situation that the individual may feel his actions of extremely small significance (and not necessarily to view them as meaningless).

The final section of this chapter looks, again, directly at the political entrepreneur. In this section his activities are examined as group size becomes larger. His viability is considered, in particular, when the environment is one in which the association is seen as defending the position of individuals in the group.´ (Such consideration follows directly from discussion of the history of the BMA).

7.1   THE POLITICAL ENTREPRENEUR

The concept of the political entrepreneur is one which has become increasingly familiar in economic and political literature. (1)   A political entrepreneur may be defined as an individual who, for personal profit, takes upon himself a part of, or all of, the costs of supplying a collective organisation and via this organisation, the provision of the collective good. He will undertake these costs provided that the total resources he can collect from the potential beneficiaries of the collective good are greater than his costs. One immediate consequence of this is that an individual may choose to occupy such a leadership role and supply a collective good to a group of individuals even if he does not value the good, or indeed even if he values the good negatively. The important consideration is that he can receive from the group resources in excess of the costs involved in his activity. (2)   It is this political surplus which the entrepreneur will attempt to maximise, and the collective good may be provided in his pursuit of this surplus. (3)

In discussions of the political entrepreneur it has been suggested that there are three main sources of finance which he may receive from beneficiaries of the collective good.(4) The first of these is referred to as extortions, in so far as the entrepreneur raises such money by his ability to threaten sanctions on his membership. The second form of payment may be that which the entrepreneur receives for private goods and services, which he provides in conjunction with the collective good. The third form of contribution is the voluntary donations made by individuals for receipt of the collective good. It is the intention to initially concentrate on this latter form of finance.

The political entrepreneur is, then, the individual who will form the association by which a collective good will be provided. He will be financed by individuals who offer donations, or in the case of the BMA, voluntarily pay membership subscriptions. Clearly, two things need to be established to continue with this line of argument. The first is that individuals will voluntarily contribute to the entrepreneur even if the collective good is non-price

exclusive. The second is that there actually is a surplus
to be made in this form of entrepreneurship.

The first proposition, i.e. that it is in the interests
of a free-rider to actually contribute to a collective good,
has been argued by A.M. Sharp and D.R. Escarraz (1964)
and has been taken up by J. Burkhead and J. Miner (1971).
Their argument may be illustrated in the following diagram.
Here the demand curves of two individuals A and B for
quantities of the collective good are shown. Individual A
finds it in his interest to provide OQ_1 of the good himself,

for his marginal evaluation of the good is greater than the
marginal cost of the good up to this output. Individual B
in the initial instance free-rides, enjoying OQ_1 at no

personal cost. Individual A would agree to pay OM per unit
if presented with the possibility of increasing the output
of the good to OQ_2. His price has dropped and yet he can
consume a greater output; his consumer surplus without

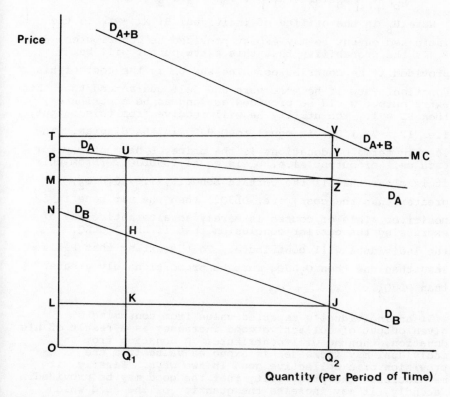

Figure 7.1 Voluntary Contribution Towards Collective Goods

question will increase. In a similar way it can be shown that individual B is also happy to contribute. Initially he enjoyed a consumer surplus of $ONHQ_1$, as his contribution was zero. Making a contribution of OL per unit he pays $OLJQ_2$ but gains consumer surplus of LNJ. Clearly if KHJ is greater than $OLKQ_1$ he is better off as a result of the contribution. The net welfare, in this partial equilibrium context, of both individuals has increased. (5)

The behaviour of individual B in the diagram can be examined more carefully. If he contributes it must be because the net expected value of so doing is positive. It is the argument of Frohlich et al that this is the important measurement which may lead individuals to contribute or not to contribute. (6) For the specific example above his expected value of contributing U_b^c may be expressed algebraically as:

$$U_b^c = \left[U_B (X_2 - X_1) \right] \cdot P_B - U_B (D_B)$$

Here U_B is the utility of individual B; $X_2 - X_1$ is the increased output he may expect provided he contributes, and P_B is the probability that this extra output will be provided if he contributes. The sum D_B is the cost of his donation. Now if he were sure and felt guaranteed that this extra output would be provided as long as he contributes, then $P_B = 1$. The utility he will receive from this output, i.e. $(X_2 - X_1) U_B$, is equal to $Q_1 HJQ_2$ in the diagram. The loss in terms of donations is the price OL he must pay for each unit of output, i.e. D_B is equal to $OLJQ_2$. From this it is clear that if the certain benefit, i.e. $Q_1 HJQ_2$, is greater than the cost, i.e. $OLJQ_2$, then the net benefit is positive. This of course is merely an alternative way of expressing the earlier conclusion that if HKJ > $OLKQ_1$ the individual will contribute. To the extent that P_B is less than one then $Q_1 HJQ_2$ must be proportionately greater than $OLJQ_2$.

If an individual's expected value from consuming a given output of collective good increases as a result of his donation, then he will contribute. A donation from an individual may increase his expected value from the provision of a collective good in two ways. Firstly, it may increase the probability that the good may be provided. Secondly, it may increase the quantity of the good which is provided. Here then lies the first important task for a political entrepreneur. He clearly has some lee-way to operate on the expectations of individuals. He might for example approach individuals and persuasively suggest that should they contribute there will be a greater certainty of the provision of a collective good. He might also suggest that should they contribute there will be a greater quantity of the good provided. The result will be to increase for the individual the expected value of donation. Obviously the donor's estimation of the probability of his contribution being significant is vital.

Whilst it has been seen that 'free-riders' can be encouraged to donate, it is still to be established that the political entrepreneur can reap a reward. He obviously requires an incentive if he is to perform the role which has just been discussed. In looking at Figure 7.1 a marginal cost sharing arrangement was implemented which meant that each individual, A and B, paid the maximum sum they were prepared to pay for the marginal unit of the good. They were charged this price per unit for the good, and in this way their consumers' surplus was larger when they both contributed to provide OQ_2 of the good. If this marginal cost sharing arrangement had been implemented by the political entrepreneur then he would have asked for contributions from A of OM per unit, and from B of OL per unit, of the collective good. The combined sums he would receive would equal $OQ_2JL + OQ_2ZM$ which is equal to OQ_2VT. Clearly then there is a surplus to be gained of PY VT over and above the costs of providing the collective good. This surplus will not be the entrepreneur's net return. The resources he collects have to cover both the costs of providing the good and also the costs of the collection organization. Even so a positive return is possible.

The appropriate marginal cost sharing arrangement will be dependent on the circumstances the entrepreneur faces. The suspicion may exist that the previous example constitutes a special case. In Figure 7.2 the problem is not as easily solvable because of the position of the two demand curves. However a marginal cost sharing arrangement is possible and collective action viable. In Figure 7.2 if B were asked to pay OL per unit, then as HJK is less than $OLKQ_1$ he would not donate, even if he felt that by so doing OQ_2 would be provided. If the entrepreneur wishes to attain a return of OT per unit to cover all costs then it is clear, given the demand functions of A and B and the initial position of B as a 'free-rider', that a simple arrangement where A pays OM and B pays OL for output OQ_2 will not be effective. The entrepreneur is able, however, to offer other alternatives. For example, assume he proposes an output increase to OQ_3. Individual A would gladly pay $OEWQ_3$ as his consumer surplus increases by PUWE. To fill the deficit of ETFW, B would pay $OGRQ_3$ which is of equal value. As a 'free-rider' B's consumer surplus is $ONHQ_1$ and

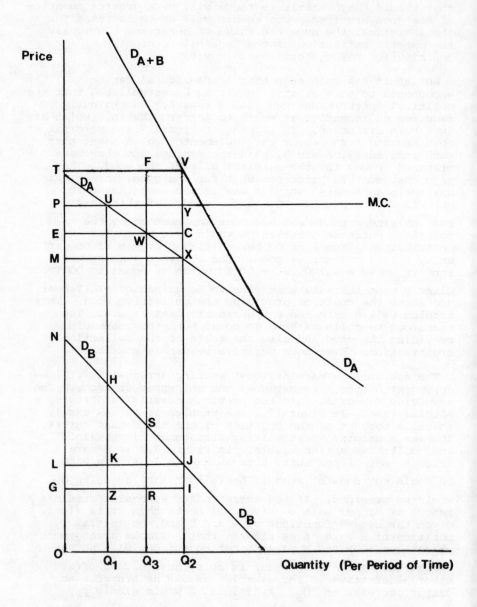

Figure 7.2 Presenting a Suitable Marginal Cost Sharing Arrangement

as a contributor it is GNSR which is greater (i.e. HSRZ > OGZQ$_1$). In such a way the political entrepreneur can increase his operations.

The scope for presenting different alternatives is extremely wide. There is no necessity that the individual pays a sum per unit which is equal to his marginal evaluation. Inasmuch as the individual is offered alternatives, the important question is whether he is better off (i.e. enjoys more consumer surplus) in the case in which he contributes. To this extent the entrepreneur has another degree of freedom. For example, consider once again a proposed output increase to OQ$_2$. Individual A would agree to pay a donation of OE per unit for an output of OQ$_2$.

Since PUWE is greater than WCX he is still prepared to contribute, for in net terms he is better off. Individual B will of course be prepared to pay OG per unit if OQ$_2$ is expected (HJIZ > OGZQ$_1$).

The option which the entrepreneur offers may reflect both his goals (e.g. output maximization or profit maximization) and his view of the attitude of the contributor. For example, the situation where A is asked to pay OE per unit for output OQ$_2$ and B is left to pay OG per unit is one which might emerge if individual A is thought "optimistic" in the high probability he attaches to a successful outcome and B "pessimistic" in the low probability he attaches to a successful outcome contingent on acceptance of the entrepreneur's offer. The consumer surplus gain for B is made proportionately greater in this case at the expense of reducing the consumer surplus gain for A. Given their assumed perceptions of the outcome following contribution this offer may prove successful where others might fail.

This short discussion of the activity of the political entrepreneur shows how flexible his options are. He may for example, enjoy prestige from organising a large association, so that his own goals need not be solely financial profit. Also by altering the marginal cost sharing arrangement he may so alter the prospective gains (in terms of consumer surplus) from one member to another that a successful arrangement may be discovered.

The significance of the donor is clearly paramount in this analysis. In small groups it will be acceptable that any individual feels of importance to the final provision of the good. The entrepreneur may indeed persuade the donor that his significance is extremely high. One technique is that referred to by Peston (1972) as the "if-then" basis for contribution. A political entrepreneur may approach a potential contributor with the inducement that if he actually contributes then it is certain that several others in the group will contribute also. The probability of that individual's subscription being effective will then appear greater. Such persuasive approaches may prove successful, but in large groups they would appear to be less viable. The question which then arises is how able is the political entrepreneur to operate as the group size increases? If, as would seem to be implied by the free-rider hypothesis of chapter four, the probability the individual attaches to his donation affecting the behaviour of others is zero, will this whole approach fail? How quickly should the "free-rider" argument be applied?

7.2   THE "FREE-RIDER" PROBLEM REVISITED

In attempting to identify exactly what is meant by the "free-rider" problem a number of possibilities exist. John McMillan (1979) surveyed the problem and argued that the "free-rider" problem is not one, but three separate problems. For example, one particular case is said to exist when individuals do not contribute enough voluntarily. to pay for a Pareto optimal quantity of the public good. Another, and more extreme, is the problem which applies when the number of agents consuming the public good becomes so large that no amount of the collective good will be contributed. Each individual refrains from contribution and in effect no one free rides. Of course, in this case one can state that individuals will not join purely for the collective good. It is to this rather strict form of the problem that attention is first turned.

In chapter four Buchanan's (1968) approach to this problem was explained. The distinction between large and small groups was crucial. In the small group case the probability that others would respond to the individual's actions was greater than zero. If the individual contributed there was a chance that others would respond by contributing more (or, indeed less). The individual's action had some effect on others. But by definition in "the large-number setting, the individual does not predict that his own behaviour can influence others in the group" (7). The individual takes the environment as given; his actions do not affect the actions of others. The example of an individual asked to contribute £5 towards the provision of a collective good which provides him with £10 value was explained in terms of the following decision matrix. If the individual feels that his contribution does not affect the actions of others then the probability (p) that others will contribute and the outcome be successful is unaffected by the decision to contribute or not to contribute. The net expected value of not contributing must then be greater than that of contributing. Whatever the value of p it must be the same in both rows of the matrix. The difference in the net expected value of contribution and non-contribution is determined solely by the size of the pay-offs; as the weights (p) and (1-p) are identical in both cases. The assumption of a large group situation keeps (p) and (1-p) identical regardless

132

of the individual's decision to contribute.

Table 7.1
The Free Rider Problem

	Others contribute	Others do not contribute
Individual contributes	£(10 - 5) (p)	£-5 (1-p)
Individual does not contribute	£10 (p)	0 (1-p)

The conclusion then rests only on the sizes of the pay-offs. Nothing is provided in the situation where the individual contributes and no one else contributes. No additional amount is provided if he contributes and all others contribute as compared with the case that others contribute and he does not. Clearly his act of contribution is also not affecting the pay-offs (except in the deduction of contribution cost); i.e. the individual does not affect total output by his contribution. Buchanan secures this result by making yet another assumption.

"In both the large-number and the small-number examples we have assumed a certain lumpiness or indivisibility in the public-goods facility. This insures that no production will be forthcoming under wholly voluntary behaviour in the large-number and perhaps in the small-number case..... If we now assume that the public good can be produced in fully divisible units, some quantity may be forthcoming even in the large-number setting. An independent-adjustment equilibrium will be established with some positive production even if this remains small relative to the Pareto optimal output under normal circumstances" (8)

The large-number situation alone does not ensure that no provision will occur under voluntary conditions. If the individual feels that his contribution leads to a change (however small) in the output that is to be provided then it is possible to pursue the following analysis. Figure 7.4 is a four quadrant diagram attempting to summarise some of the inter-relationships embodied in the provision of a collective good which is divisible in production. The demand function for individual A is illustrated in quadrant 1 and that for an identical individual, i.e. B, in quadrant 11. Individual B's demand will depend on whether or not A provides any of the good. If he does then B will enjoy that provision also and hence reduce his demand for the good accordingly. The same applies for individual A. Initially the solid line demand functions are drawn for B (and for A) on the assumption

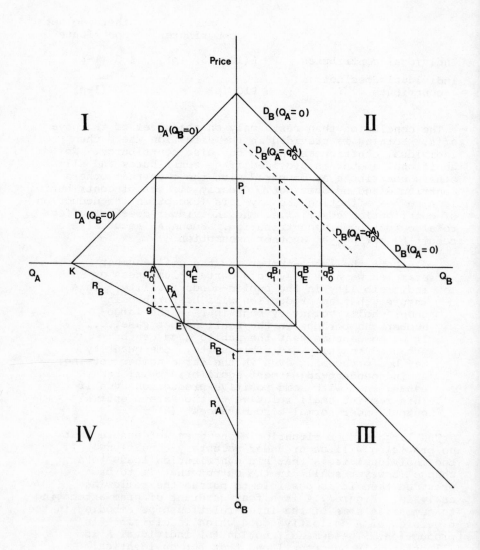

Figure 7.3 Independent Adjustment of the Provision of Collective Goods

that the other provides none of the good. In this case, if
B were faced with a price of P_1, then he would demand
q_o^B (and similarly A would purchase q_o^A).

If individual B were to find that instead of A providing
nothing of the collective good he instead provided a total
amount of q_o^A, then one would expect B's demand to be
reduced. As q_o^A is equal to the amount q_o^B then B could
economise by consuming that quantity provided by A. His
demand curve would shift to the left but would it be the
case that he would now wish to purchase nothing? If he has
received Oq_o^A of the good free his real income will have
risen and if the good is normal he will still consume a
positive amount. Hence the demand function shifts back only
as far as D_B ($Q_A = q_o^A$) and, when A provides q_o^A, B still
provides q_1^B. (9)

In quadrant III the insertion of a 45 degree line enables
a straightforward transformation of B's quantity from the
horizontal to the vertical axis. So that in quadrant IV one
can plot the corresponding quantities B demands (e.g. q_1^B)
for given quantities provided by A (e.g. q_o^A). A locus of
points such as g may then be identified as the reaction
function $R_B R_B$. This shows B's quantity provided for
quantities A chooses to provide. The slope of this function
will depend on the income effect. If the income effect is
normal then distance OK exceeds ot (i.e. the absolute value
of the slope OK/ot > 1).

The same procedure can be applied for individual A and
$R_A R_A$ will indicate those quantities A chooses to provide for
given quantities provided by B. If each individual assumes
the other will continue to provide the same amount of the
collective good irrespective of his own action, an
adjustment procedure will lead to an equilibrium outcome.
The equilibrium outcome will be that A provides q_E^A and B
provides q_E^B. (10)

The interesting question is whether the total ($q_E^A + q_E^B$)
will fall as the size of the group increases. Following
Chamberlin (1974) we redraw B's reaction function in
Figure 7.4. On the vertical axis for Q_a we write $q(n-1)$
where n is the number of individuals in the group. The
total is $q_E^B + q_E^{(n-1)}$. As n increases and $q(n-1)$ increases
then q^B will fall. However, because the slope of the
function OK/ot exceeds one in absolute value (or indeed is

135

less than -1), as q (n-1) increases q^B falls by a smaller amount and hence total provision increases. (11). Everything depends on the slope of the reaction function. If the income effect is normal then as the value of n increases the total provision of the good increases. Each individual's contribution falls but the total contribution increases, (only literally when the size of the group is infinity will each contribution equal zero.) Hence, as the good is non-excludable but divisible in production, an independent adjustment mechanism shows that for a group of identical individuals total provision of a collective good increases as numbers increase. (We do not argue that this kind of independent adjustment leads to Pareto Optimality. Elsewhere, see for example M. Pauly (1970), it has been shown to be less than such an output. For our purposes it suffices to show it positive and, in total, increasing as numbers increase.)

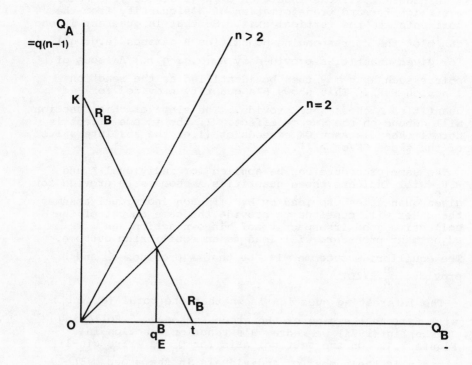

Figure 7.4 Equilibrium for Different Group Sizes

The case of the public good which is divisible is one
where the political entrepreneur may operate. The object
of the political entrepreneur is then to convey the
impression that the contribution of each member to the
association will add at the margin to total output. The
task may, of course, not be easy; but attempts to pursue it
are evident. For example, charities raising funds for
developing countries have adopted the strategy of linking
the donor's contribution directly to the welfare of a
particular individual in an overseas developing country.
The objective is to show the donor how his contribution has
effect. Similarly periodic publicity shows how sums of
money (or goods and services) provided, grow with additional
contribution. Tullock (1966) has described how, by skilful
use of information supplied to contributors, an entrepreneur
might lead them to believe they were effective as a result
of additional contribution. Donors to associations may be
informed exactly how much extra can be provided for
different sums which they choose to contribute.
Convalescent homes may tell the donor that for alternative
sums which are donated alternative items can be purchased.
The impression is given that at the margin something extra
can be provided as a result of donation. In the case of
union negotiation the problem may be more difficult. The
adjustment at the margin may be less perceptible. But why
should a subscriber not believe that, however small it may
be, his contribution will add something to make the union
more strong? It may be difficult to perceive and measure,
but does this automatically imply it is zero? However
inefficient it may be, individuals may equate inputs to an
association with output, and a rise in the one may be
thought to imply a potential rise in the other. The studies
of the CBI and the BMA showed the members' prime interest was
in the negotiating task. Is it fair to assume that each
subscription adds nothing to the strength of the negotiating
body even though one would be at pains to measure precisely
the addition? Certainly the political entrepreneur will
refrain from giving the impression that their contribution
adds nothing.

It is true that in certain circumstances, even if
divisibility in production is assumed, the free-rider
dilemma can still emerge. The above analysis has assumed
that the good was both non-excludable and non-rival in
consumption. By relaxing the assumption that the good is
non-rival in consumption the distinction Olson made
between "inclusive" and "exclusive" goods is valid. (12)
The former refer to situations when non-rivalness is
assumed and the latter to those cases where this is not
the case. In the latter case it is possible,given the
benefit to cost ratio and the numbers in the group,to fall
into another version of the "prisoner's dilemma" game.(13)

Take the example of a collective good which is provided
to two individuals. Each is asked to pay 1 unit and, for
a total cost of 2 units, a good worth collectively 3 units
is provided. The good is rival in consumption so that each

person benefits to the extent of 1.5 units. The good is divisible in production so that if only one person subscribes he can expect that for the total contribution of 1 unit a good with a collective benefit of 1.5 units (and individual benefit of 0.75 units) will be provided (i.e. constant costs of provision of the good). In the following Table 7.2 the choice open to the two individuals is as follows:

Table 7.2
The "Prisoner's Dilemma" Problem

		Individual B	
		Contribute	Not contribute
Individual A	Contribute	+0.5, +0.5	-0.25, +0.75
	Not contribute	+0.75,-0.25	+0 0

In this case, where the pay-offs to A and B can be read in each cell from left to right respectively, there is a presumption that neither individual will contribute. Whatever the other individual does the pay-offs from the strategy of non-contribution dominate those from contribution.

Even though the individual's contribution leads to an increase in output the problem of the "free-rider" has reappeared. But it is not exactly the same problem that was analysed in chapter four. The fact that the individual can affect outcomes because the good is divisible in production means that there remain circumstances in which he might contribute. One possibility is the introduction of altruism. Assume that individual B's pay-offs affect A's happiness (i.e. that B's utility enters A's utility function). Assume that he weights B's pay-offs by a factor V and his own by a factor (1-V). In the case of pure selfish behaviour $V = 0$ and the net expected value of not contributing exceeds that of contribution. However $V = \frac{1}{2}$ and clearly the ordering is reversed. (14) Such a possibility exists in this type of problem even though it did not exist when the good was thought indivisible in production. If the individual's contribution does absolutely nothing to change output then, of course, however he weights his utility and that of others, it is futile to incur the costs of contribution.

The above possibility of a "prisoner's dilemma" kind can arise when the good is thought to be divisible in production. Note that it occurs when the good is rival in consumption and that it depends on benefit to cost ratios as well as the size of the group. (15) The result is not assured.

The assumption of indivisibility in the production of the collective good is therefore a very important assumption in explaining the extreme position of the Buchanan "free-rider" problem. There are situations in which one might wish to keep this assumption. Even if it is assumed, it is still possible to argue that yet another implicit assumption is working behind the scenes to ensure the prediction that the individuals choose not to contribute. The individual must consider that <u>all</u> future possibilities are either that no one else contributes, (S_1), or that sufficient contribution is made to affect successful increase in output, (S_2). But why should the individual believe the future contains only two possibilities. We could consider introducing just one more future possibility (S_i).

In S_i not all non-members contribute but a large proportion do. In fact so many contribute that they are just one donation away from the amount required to produce the good. The individual's contribution is no longer intra-marginal but is significant. Below assume the good is worth £11 to the individual and he is asked to donate £5. The pay offs for each outcome are

Table 7.3
Increasing the Possibilities

	S_1	S_i	S_2
C	-5	11-5	11-5
NC	0	0	11

It is now impossible to predict the decision of the individual. If he follows a maximin strategy he still does not contribute as this is the best choice if S_1, the worst outcome, occurred. However, he might yet choose a minimax regret criterion. The approach here is to protect the individual against excessive cost of mistakes. The regret matrix below is constructed from Table 7.3.

Table 7.4
A Regret Matrix

	S_1	S_i	S_2
C	5	0	5
NC	0	6	0

The choice is then the strategy which minimizes the regret element. As this occurs above with contribution then he avoids non-contribution which could yield the greatest mistake. (16)

Of course both the maximin and the minimax regret criterion can be objected to in that the decision is made on the basis of one future possibility only. They are applied in the face of perfect uncertainty. If, however, the individual has an idea or hunch as to the relative likelihood of each he can weigh them by a subjectively held probability. Whether situations like S_i are likely or widely possible is not argued for the moment. We can move on to consider the factors that make such occurrences possible (i.e. where the individual has marginal significance even though in average terms he may appear extremely unimportant). For the moment it is necessary to note that in our earlier discussion these cases had implicitly been dismissed. Without explanation the likelihood of their occurrence was taken to be zero.

The above example can be thought of in terms of Figure 7.1. In constraining the future possibilities the individual would not voluntarily participate in collective action. If individual B was asked to donate and had no idea how other individuals behave he could question the decision in the following manner. He might say that the discrete jump in output which is proposed (i.e. OQ_1 to OQ_2) will not occur if he alone contributes. Secondly, if all others contribute sufficient (i.e. OQ_2 VT) it will be forthcoming whether or not he contributes. Yet there may be at least another possibility. That all others (in this case A) contribute OQ_2 ZM and his donation of OQ_2 JL will be just enough to bring about the increase. In this situation his contribution is marginal. Indeed for all those contributions by others between OQ_2 VT and OQ_2 ZM his contribution will ensure success in terms of the increase in output. There are cases then when the expected value of his contribution is positive and it is somewhat arbitrary to limit the future to those cases where it is not.

This example is only one wherein the individual can be significant in his actions. There are many other such cases where the individual might believe beforehand that his contribution may just prove effective. Stigler (1974) in his examination of trade associations pointed to the possibility that the output of the collective good varies as a result of the type of membership. He distinguished between small and large firms. The small firms produced a narrower range of products than the large and clearly if they are not in the association the possibility exists that its time and effort will be devoted to aims that do

140

not benefit them. As Stigler puts it, "if they are not
represented in the coalition they may find that their cheap
ride is to a destination they do not favour. The proposed
tariff structure may neglect their products; the research
program may neglect their processes; the labour
negotiations may ignore their special mix". (17)

In the following example: $\not{s}_i$ = the share of sales of
commodity i made by the combined large firms; $(1 - \not{s}_i)$ =
the share of sales made by the combined small firms; S_i =
the total sales of commodity i; $S_L S_8$ = the total sales
of large and small firms, respectively; $S_L + S_8$ = S which
is total sales. The relative importance of sales of
commodity i to the large firm is $\frac{\not{s}_i S_i}{S_L}$, and hence the
difference between large and small firms in this relative
importance is $\Delta_i = S_i \cdot \left[\frac{\not{s}_i}{S_L} - \frac{(1 - \not{s}_i)}{S_8} \right]$. Stigler refers
to this as the measure of the discordance of interest
between large and small firms. Given that k = the share of
total sales made by large firms (i.e. k (the concentration

ratio) = $\frac{S_L}{S_L + S_8}$)   this can be re-written

$\Delta_i = \frac{S_i}{S} \cdot \left[\frac{\not{s}_i}{k} - \frac{(1 - \not{s}_i)}{1 - k} \right]$ If such a measure is
sufficiently large, Stigler believes it will bring firms
into the association.

The fact then that the decisions which are made are rival
even though the output when produced may be non-rival is
significant. As has been argued in chapter two, general
practitioners and hospital doctors share common goals, but
there are clearly issues which will be of greater
importance to one sub-set of doctors than to the other.
If, given the constitution of the association, decisions
as to the use of resources between these issues depend on
the predominance of different sub-sets, the individual may
feel inclined to join. The probability that an individual
will have some effect on the use of resources depends on
the different sub-sets within the associaton and on how
close the final decision is likely to be. The closer the
outcome the greater the probability that his membership
will count. The crucial element is not simply the absolute
membership, but rather whether an extra member for one sub-
group may help swing the decision. That is to say one
should not concentrate on average measures at the expense
of marginal considerations.

Such an approach has been applied in explaining
electoral turn-out in the USA. In this large number

setting, voter participation was related to the closeness
of elections. By assuming that the ex-post winning
majority is a proxy for the anticipated (ex-ante) outcome
Barzel and Silberger (1973) found such a variable was
significant in explaining turn-out. Silberman and Durden
(1975), looking at congressional elections in the USA
arrived at the same conclusion. In the case of the BMA
to the extent that the GPA, JHDA and HCSA have acted as
"ginger groups" membership of these associations may be
viewed in terms of doctors wishing to increase the likely
effect they may have on decisions. (That is to say that
membership of such associations increases the likelihood of
state of nature S_i in Table 7.3).

In looking back at these 'escapes' to the free-rider the
review presented is not exhaustive. For example it
concentrates on the situation where the decision to
contribute or not contribute is taken on a one-off basis.
It is of course possible to consider successive
consideration of such a decision and its effect on the
other players. Hence the construction of "Supergames".
Co-operative behaviour in such circumstances may be even
more likely. (18) In this study however attention has
focused on the large number situation where the individual
reacts to a given situation and does not believe that by
strategically altering his decision to contribute in a
successive number of situations he will affect the
behaviour of others. (Indeed in the BMA case the evidence
of the previous chapter suggests doctors seldom stop to
reappraise a decision to contribute). At the time of
joining he may have some guess as to what others may do
and then act accordingly. But after the event it is rare
for a reappraisal to be made. Even so within this
limitation the survey suggests the following taxonomy of
cases. These situations are characterised for large number
situations according to whether or not the non-excludable
good is indivisible in production and rival in consumption.

Table 7.5
A Taxonomy of "Free-Rider" Problems

	Non-Rival	Rival
Divisible	B	C
Indivisible	A	D

Clearly Buchanan's free-rider example would tend to fall
into category A. In our sequence we discussed the
possibility in B that when group size increased total
provision of a collective good may increase rather than
fall though each individual may individually provide less.
In C the problem of group size and free-riding occurs
inasmuch as the total good provided must be shared amongst

142

those in the group. However the problem is not inevitable.
It may depend upon the benefit-cost ratio and numbers in
the group. Even when it occurs assumptions of altruism
may explain contribution (though the same assumption need
not similarly work in category A.)

Finally it is possible to consider the case above where
the good is indivisible in production but the decision on
its provision or an alternative is rival. In this
way it is possible that an outcome occurs where the
individual's actions may have an effect (and for example,
given a minimax regret rule this may lead him to
contribute).

If all of these possibilities exist the equation of
the strict free-rider result with the provision of non-
excludable goods is questionable even though the size of
the group is large. In this light it is perhaps not
surprising to see people behave as if they have some
possible impact on the provision of collective goods.
Peter Bohm's (1972) experiment, for example, illustrates
this. A random sample of individuals were drawn from the
population of Stockholm. The subjects were divided into
six groups and were given the impression that there were
many groups of the same size simultaneously being asked
questions. They were asked how much they would pay to
watch a television program, and were told that provided
the sum stated exceeded the costs the program would be
shown. (19)   Each of the six groups were told that there
would be different implications for financing the proposal.
Group One were told that each would be asked to pay the
amount stated. Group Five were told the costs would be
paid by the taxpayers in general. Each group was informed
of the strategies and counter strategies they might pursue.
Group One were told that by stating a small amount they
stood the chance of being able to watch the program without
paying so much. But also that if all, or many, pursued
this venture the total would not reach the necessary sum
and the program would not be shown. Similarly Group Five
were told that "it would pay for any one of you who really
wanted to watch this program to state a much higher amount
than he would actually be willing to pay", but that this,
for example, "would indicate a lack of solidarity or
respect for the views of your neighbours, who may be
called upon to pay for something that is not really desired
by all of you together". (20)   In this way it was put as
something of a 'duty' to state the amount they actually
found it worth to see the program.

The role of the interviewer then might be considered
similar to that of a political entrepreneur to the extent
that counter strategies were also put. One result which
became apparent was that the responses of Group One and
Five revealed no significant differences (at the 5 per cent
level). In fact it was claimed that "Our main result,
however, is that the reactions received from the different

143

groups are compatible with the possibility of getting
identical responses to instructions I to V. This possible
interpretation would either mean that people do not use
available "cheating strategies" even when made explicit or
that the "counter-strategic" arguments ..... and the moral
arguments ..... as well as the general feature of non-
anonymity, neutralises tendencies to use such strategies.
The possibility that instruction I could after all reveal
actual preferences for a public good conforms to the view
sometimes advocated that people tend to regard their
impact on total demand, however small it may be, as
"important"."(21)

7.3 "DEFENSIVE" AND "PROMOTIONAL" ASSOCIATIONS

In the previous section the case has been made that
individuals may believe that they have some influence on
events even as numbers get larger. While they may not
believe their action can directly affect the behaviour of
others, their contributions can in certain cases affect
total output of associations. If the good is divisible in
production an extra contribution can possibly affect total
provision at the margin. The individual may feel that
there is just a chance that such an outcome exists no matter
how remote this may be. The effectiveness of the
association might just be influenced in a marginal way by
an extra contribution. Also, if this possibility is
certain to be closed and the good is strictly indivisible
(in the sense that a certain output will either be produced
or not produced) there is yet the possibility that an
individual's membership of the association might bring some
influence on the type or quality of the good provided.
Such cases may be debatable but empirical evidence does
suggest that individuals feel that their contribution may
count for something. The expected value of contribution
may be positive.

It is in the light of such arguments that one can proceed,
under the above definition of large groups, with the view
that political entrepreneurship can operate on the expected
value of contribution. An individual has a number of
reasons to believe that there are conditions in which he
may just influence events. Factors such as the possibility
of divisibility in production of the good, the proportional
composition of the association and its constitution and the
size of the group are all relevant. (22) Subjectively
the individual holds a belief that there is a probability
that he can influence events. In much the same way as when
purchasing a raffle ticket in a lottery he is aware that he
has a remote possibility of winning, the individual
similarly is led to gamble that his contribution will have
an effect when he joins the association. He believes his
real income may just possibly be greater than that which
it would otherwise have been if he did not take this action
(that others also could be affected will not influence him;

only the size of the expected gain to him relative to his costs of membership). The role of the political entrepreneur can be seen in the way in which he reduces the real costs of individuals taking this gamble inherent in membership of associations.

Assume an individual has a certain income X and he considers the chance of contributing to an association in the hope that this will lead to an increase in his income level to (X + Z). The individual's choice as between accepting or refusing can be analysed. He is indifferent when:

$$U_i (X) = p_i \left[U_i (X + Z) - U_i(D_i) \right] + (1 - p_i) \left[U_i(X) - U_i(D_i) \right]$$

... (7.2)

$U_i(X)$ = the utility of individual i for a certain income of X

p_i = the probability individual i feels that his donation will affect the outcome

$U_i(X+Z)$ = individual i's utility when the association is successful

$U_i(D_i)$ = the utility of the donation

For values of X, Z and D there will be a critical value of p_i at which the individual will be indifferent to the gamble and above which he will choose the gamble.

The political entrepreneur clearly has a difficult task in large groups where for any individual the view he takes of his significance is likely to be extremely small. Though it is subjective and dependent on the variables outlined above, it is unlikely that any individual will feel extremely important. If the critical value of p_i in the equation above exceeded the subjective value (p), which the individual holds of the chances of his donation proving successful, then the individual would not take the gamble. His subjective view of his importance would be smaller than the importance which his action must have to make the gamble worthwhile. The problem to the entrepreneur is to make the gamble acceptable even though the individual feels the chances of his contribution leading to success are extremely small.

The use of the selective incentive can be viewed in just this light. It makes the net expected value of the gamble greater for any value of p_i. It makes the gamble worthwhile even when individuals feel of little significance. Below the necessary conditions for the individual to be indifferent as to the decision to take the gamble becomes

145

$$U_i(X) = p_i \left[U_i(X + Z) + U_i(S_i) - U_i(D_i) \right] + \ldots\ldots$$
$$\ldots (1-p_i) \left[U_i(X) + U_i(S_i) - U_i(D_i) \right] \ldots\ldots \quad (7.3)$$

where S_i = a selective incentive which is enjoyed
independently of the collective good.

One aspect of this argument which bears on the analysis
of the BMA and the role of selective incentives is the
existence of a "threat". A "threat" can be defined as a
situation which occurs so as to lead the individual to
believe that his current way of life is insecure. That is
to say, in our example, the individual may enjoy an income
of X but if he feels threatened he will not regard this as
his "certain" level of income. His "certain" level of
income will be lower. More will be said of this definition
of threat and its relationship to the workings of the
market in the following chapter. At present we continue
on the basis that under "threat" conditions the certain
level of income to the individual is less than the current
level.

Figure 7.5 simply illustrates an individual's choice
under uncertainty. He is offered either a certain income
Y_c (£10) or by paying a donation (£5), a fifty fifty chance
of gaining an income Y_p (£20). (The net expected income of
the gamble being $\frac{1}{2}(20-5) + \frac{1}{2}(10-5) = £10$). The utility
function is concave from below and reflects diminishing
marginal utility of income. The expected utility of the
risk situation is $\frac{1}{2}U(20-5) + \frac{1}{2}U(10-5)$ and this will be
lower than $U(10)$, as by assumption the function is concave
from below. The individual will therefore not accept a
"fair" gamble where the net expected income equals his
certain income. If however, the probability of
successfully attaining Y_p increased such that Y* were the
net expected income of the gamble, he would be indifferent.
If p were greater then he would accept the gamble. (23)

Figure 7.6 takes this a step further in order to
illustrate the distinction between "threatened" and "safe"
environments. Typically the contributions to associations
(i.e. D) are not great. Initially in an unthreatened
world his current income is his secure or certain income
level and hence his reference point. If he is asked to
choose between Y_c and $p(Y_p -D) + (1-p)(Y_c -D)$ he will take
the latter only if p is equal to or greater than that value
which makes Y_1^* the expected income. However, if he is in
a "threatened" world, then by definition Y_c is not his
secure income. His secure income is less. (In the last
round he may have been fortunate to receive Y_c but this is
now not his secure position because he is threatened). If

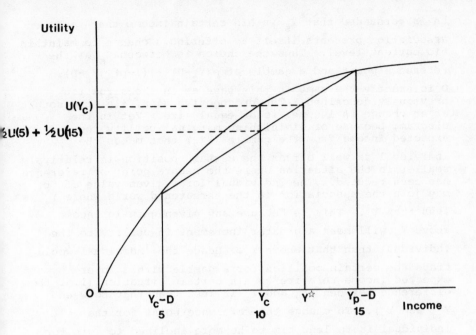

Figure 7.5   Expected Utility: A Risk Averse Utility Function

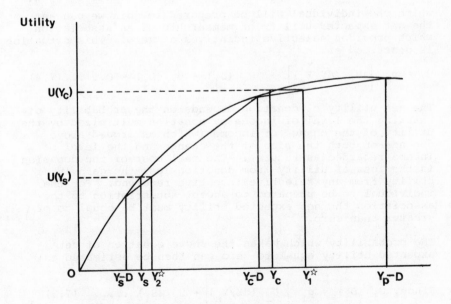

Figure 7.6   Defensive and Promotional Situations

he is persuaded that Y_s is his certain income the association presents itself as offering a chance to maintain his current level. Thus the choice is between Y_s as the reference point and a gamble of $p(Y_c-D) + (1-p)(Y_s-D)$. D is exactly the same in this case as in the situation previously described. The prospective gain, i.e. the sought after change in income, is of equal size. Yet in the diagram, because of diminishing marginal utility the expected income from the gamble $(Y*_2)$ that makes the individual as well off as the certain position is relatively smaller in the situation where the secure point of reference has been reduced. The individual for a given value of p may join the association in the threatened world where Y_s is less than Y_c. This is because any given gain in income above Y_s will mean a greater increment in utility to the individual than that above Y_c. Hence the individual would trade the certain position for a gamble with a lower expected income relative to his certain situation (i.e. the difference between $Y*_2$ and Y_s is less than that between $Y*_1$ and Y_c). To change the reference point for the individual is to lead him to be more inclined to join for any value he may have of his effectiveness. This we relate to the BMA in the next chapter. (24)

In order to discuss further the critical value of p_i at which the individual will be prepared to join we can set the net expected utility of membership of an association which provides selective incentives at zero. This situation is described as:

$$U_i = p_i \left[U_i \ (dY/Y_s) \right] + U_i \ (S_i) - U_i \ (D_i) = 0 \ldots\ldots (7.4)$$

The net utility of donation depends on the probability of changing the level of income by donation multiplied by the utility of the change of income (which as argued above depends on both the size of the change and the level of income regarded as secure). The real cost of the donation is the loss of utility from donation less the gain in utility from any selective incentive received. For the individual to be prepared to accept subscription to the association the net expected utility must be equal to or greater than zero.

The probability which makes the above equation of net expected utility equal to zero can then be estimated as:

$$\text{Since, } U_i \ (D_i) = p_i \left[U_i \ (dY/Y_s) \right] + U_i \ (S_i) \ldots.. (7.5)$$

148

then $$\frac{U_i(D_i) - U_i(S_i)}{U_i(dY/Y_s)} = p_i \qquad \ldots\ldots (7.6)$$

It is the case that p_i can be reduced by a careful selection of activities by the political entrepreneur. For an association,which sets out to attain a collective good and hence increase the level of income (dY) of individuals, a number of alternatives are open to the political entrepreneur who wishes to reduce p_i. Increasing the value of the selective incentive (S_i) is obviously a possibility. If the value of D_i could be reduced this would lead to the same result. Associations invariably explore ways by which tax relief, for example, can be gained on subscriptions. Barry Keating (1977) discusses the special tax status on pressure groups.which is conferred by the Internal Revenue Code in the USA. Finally, it is clear that the lower is Y_s the higher the value of the denominator and the lower the value of p_i. If political entrepreneurs can persuade people that they are threatened, i.e. that their current income level is above their secure level, then this makes the gamble for potential members more attractive. In order to do this, events which individuals perceive will be interpreted by the political entrepreneur as "threats". Keating (1977) has noted that individuals will band together in response to a "threat" and, to the extent that this is relaxed, inducements of a selective incentive nature will be required to keep them in the association. R. Salisbury (1969) looked to cases in America where Farmers' Associations have not depended so heavily on selective incentives when a collectively felt threat existed. Studies of unions, such as that of E.J. Dvorak (1962), point to the existence of ephemeral associations which exist in response to a threat and for which individuals will not maintain membership after the liquidation of the threat. These studies, by no means exhaustive, suggest a trade-off between action on S_i and Y_s to attract membership. What is clear is that they may both be applied simultaneously in some "optimum" combination to attract membership to associations.

In this way, though the individual may feel of very small importance, the entrepreneur may offer a gamble in which only a very small chance of changing the outcome (i.e. attaining the collective good) is necessary to lead him to purchase the gamble. It may be the case that in small groups the entrepreneur's main line of approach is to persuade the individual that his effectiveness (p) is greater than he thought, by, for example, showing how others would follow his lead. In larger groups the emphasis changes to that of making the critical value of the gamble p as low as possible by such strategies as outlined above.

AN ASSESSMENT

In this chapter three related aspects of the provision of collective goods have been discussed. Firstly, the case has been established that a political entrepreneur can mobilise collective action. Free-riders can be induced to contribute and political entrepreneurs can at the same time earn a private reward. The argument however hangs on the donor believing that the expected value of contribution is positive.

The second part of this chapter looked at the assumptions required to ensure that the individual would not believe the expected value of contribution was positive. To ensure instead that it is zero the individual must believe that his action is completely impotent. This is dependent not only on assumptions concerning the size of the group, but also on the nature of the good. The assumption is necessary that the good be considered indivisible in production. In large groups, by definition, individuals cannot influence other individuals' behaviour. However if the good is divisible they can affect total output by their action. To the extent that individuals contribute they may feel that this makes the association more effective at the margin. Hence, rightly or wrongly, they may deem the expected value of their action greater than zero. Furthermore, even when the good is indivisible or "lumpy" in production they must consider that ex ante their membership will not affect the quality of the good provided. The future is seen simply in terms of a given good being provided or not provided and this is not influenced by their membership. If instead there is just a remote chance that they will influence the type of good provided then they cannot be assumed to believe that the expected value of contribution is zero. The question is then raised as to whether all the assumptions required to ensure the expected value to be zero do not represent a special case? Is it more general to assume that even in groups where one individual's behaviour does not affect the behaviour of others (i.e. large groups) the individual may consider the expected value associated with his action to be small but positive? Empirically Peter Bohm's (1972) experiment reveals that individuals behave as if their actions are "important" not "impotent".

A rather fuller examination then of the "free-rider" hypothesis does raise this doubt and in the light of this the political entrepreneur's behaviour is discussed in a somewhat larger group setting. After all, when approached by such an organiser is it not arguable that the fact that the individual is being canvassed for support will not lead him to believe that his support counts for something? In a large group the political entrepreneur presents a package which by judicious use of selective incentives reduces the net cost of taking a chance that contribution will lead to something. If, for the reasons argued above, the individual thinks there is just a chance that his contribution is of importance he may contribute; in the same way as the

purchase of a lottery ticket may be related to a vague
possibility of winning. The costs of contribution, or
taking the membership gamble, are kept low by tax relief on
donation and the assured receipt of selective incentives.
The attraction of the gamble is also greater when the
entrepreneur is seen as defending a given income rather than
pursuing an additional income. If the
marginal utility of income is diminishing the expected
utility of the former situation will be greater for any
probability that donation will be effective.

The following chapter is designed to take up the argument
that doctors have considered the role of the BMA as
primarily "defensive". If the intervention of government
has led them to feel "threatened" and if they appear to
behave as though the expected utility of action is not
zero (25), then the BMA by presenting a package which keeps
the costs of membership low will be likely to experience
growth. Such growth will be correlated with increasing
insecurity and "threat". (26)

NOTES

1   See for example Robert H Salisbury (1969), A. Breton
    and R. Breton, (1969) and particularly Norman Frolich
    Joe A. Oppenheimer, Oran R. Young, (1971)
2   These costs could include the opportunity costs of the
    individual, i.e. how much he might have received in
    his next best occupation.
3   This political surplus could of course contain non-
    pecuniary as well as pecuniary items. That is to say
    that part of the return may be the feeling of power
    and prestige that leadership may bring.
4   See Frohlich et al (1971)
5   Sharp and Escarraz (1964) argue that individuals will
    reveal preferences rather than go without the good
    because they are better off by so doing. They directly
    challenge Musgrave's argument that preferences will not
    be revealed even in the large group. Escarraz (1966)
    directly takes up the argument. He takes as an
    example of this the work of Charles M. Tiebout (1955).
    Tiebout found that individuals would move from a low
    rateable value area to one which had higher rates, but
    improved amenities. Thus they appear to be guided
    by the value which they got from rates rather than a
    straightforward desire to keep rates low. As such it
    appears that individuals would be prepared and would
    choose to pay more if the quantity of collective goods
    were increased.
6   N. Frohlich et al (1971), p.32
7   J.M. Buchanan (1968), p.89
8   J.M. Buchanan (1968), p.91
9   This type of equilibrium is akin to a "Cournot"
    solution. Each individual adjusts the amount he
    provides on the assumption that the other does not

alter his behaviour. The Cournot assumption is so named after Augustin Cournot who analysed this kind of inter-dependence in 1838.

10 See, for example, A. Williams (1966)

11 This analysis is based on that of John Chamberlin (1974) As can be seen the total amount of the good provided is equal to the sum of the horizontal and vertical components of the equilibrium $nq_E^i = q_E^i + (n-1) q_E^i$. If the reaction curve is stated as a function of q^i (say $F(q^i)$ then $nq_E^i = q_E^i + F(q_E^i)$. The derivative of this function with respect to q_E^i is

$$\frac{d(q_E^i + F(q_E^i))}{dq_E^i} = 1 + F^1 (q_E^i)$$

If $F^1(q_E^i)$ is less than -1 (i.e. the good is normal in terms of the income effect) then the amount of the good provided increases as q_E^i decreases. Hence the amount of the good provided by the group increases as group size increases.

12 M. Olson, Jr. (1971) p.36

13 See M. Bacharach (1976)

14 See D. Collard (1978). Note that in Table 7.2, in the case of an assurance gamble, where each expects the other to contribute, the value of V need only equal $\frac{1}{4}$ for individual A to be prepared to contribute.

15 See Russel Hardin (1971)

16 For example John A. Ferejohn and P. Fiorina (1974)

17 G. Stigler (1974), p.362

18 See, for example, A. Rapaport and A.M. Chammah (1965); M. Taylor (1976); and J. McMillan (1979)

19 P. Bohm (1972). Note the questionnaire should imply that the individual would lose if the programme was not shown if the example accords to the strict "free-rider" problem

20 P. Bohm (1972), p.129

21 P. Bohm (1972), p.124. Note that political sociologists have shown that individuals feel significant in large group situations, e.g. G.A. Almond and S. Verba (1965)

22 See, for example, N. Frohlich and J.A. Oppenheimer (1970)

23 M. Friedman and L.J. Savage (1948)

24 Buchanan (1968) argues that in threat situations large groups behave as small groups because the individual's subjective value of his significance increases in such circumstances. E.g. "There is, of course, no a priori means of determining just what size a group must be in order to bring about the basic shift in any individual's behaviour pattern. This will vary from one individual to another, even for members of the same group. The critical limit is imposed by the

personal relationship that the individual feels with his fellows in negotiation. During periods of extreme stress, such as was apparently evidenced by the British during World War II, behaviour characteristic of small groups may have extended over almost the whole population. In other situations, when such cohesive forces do not exist and when commonly-shared goals are not apparent, individuals may behave as they would in large groups even for quite limited community actions. Variations in custom, tradition, in ethical standards, all these serve to shift the critical limits between small group and large group behaviour".

25   Take, for example, the survey D. Mechanic and R.G. Faich (1970) made at the time of the controversy between the Ministry of Health and general practitioners in 1965. On the basis of replies from 1,365 of the 1,500 general practitioners chosen at random, they were able to show that those who had a greater personal stake in the issues at hand were more ready to support a strike. Doctors were more ready, then, to take action the larger the expected benefit to them. If they regarded the significance of their action as zero then the expected benefit would be zero regardless, and this result would not emerge.

26   As a final note on the impact of the "threat" situation the following comparison shows that, where individuals do not pursue an estimate of net expected value but instead apply an alternative decision making rule, the case is distinctly different. In Table 7.6 the pay-offs correspond to an individual asked to contribute £5 for the attainment of a collective good worth £10. In Table 7.7 he is asked to contribute £5 to produce a collective good, defence, which avoids a loss of £10. Assume the marginal utility of money is constant. In Table 7.7 pursuit of a maximin strategy leads to the observation that in the worst outcome the costs of contribution are infinitely higher than those of non-contribution. The zero appearing in the bottom left hand corner reflects a safe positon and for a maximin strategist makes any other action than non-contribution infinitely more expensive. Yet in Table 7.8 if the worst outcome occurs he must lose in any case and in relative terms loses one and half times as much by contribution. The significance of contribution costs are reduced. True a strict application of the maximin strategy leads to non-contribution in both cases; but are they really identical? Will the latter not offer greater scope for a political entrepreneur?

Table 7.7
Contribution to a Promotional Association

	Others contribute	Others do not contribute
contribute	£(10 - 5)	£ (- 5)
not contribute	£10	0

Table 7.8
Contribution to a Defensive Association

	Others contribute	Others do not contribute
contribute	£(- 5)	£ (- 15)
not contribute	0	£ (- 10)

8 Conclusions

One theme that has pervaded this analysis of the BMA is the response of a group of individuals to the threat which they may consider to be associated with the advent of significant changes in the market in which they sell their skills. A review of the history of the BMA indicated this response to be a greater willingness to participate in collective action. To the extent that the gains from collective action were non-excludable, such a response did not fit easily with the typical predictions of collective choice theory. Whether the Association defended or promoted the welfare of doctors the result was non-excludable to non-members and the prediction of 'free-riding' might be expected.

Yet this study reflects an asymmetry in the willingness to participate according to whether individuals feel secure or threatened. The BMA appears to have assumed the role of a defensive association. If doctors are not completely convinced that their contribution must count for nothing, then it can be argued that they may take the gamble associated with subscription to an association. If an association offers other certain excludable benefits the costs attendant on the gamble are reduced. These excludable benefits may not totally compensate for the costs of subscription, and members may still require to feel the common goal is to be pursued. As such there may just be a remote possibility that their contribution may affect the quality or quantity of the outcome. In such conditions it is likely that a threat will lead to greater participation. A threat being defined as a situation where the individual believes that his current level of income is significantly above his secure level of income. That is to say, if doctors felt that within the market they could substitute so as to change their activities and maintain their welfare then there would be no threat. However, if individual action of this sort can only lead to a reduced level, then they may feel themselves threatened.

8.1   THE BMA AS A "DEFENSIVE" ASSOCIATION

Professor Abel-Smith has noted that: "Doctors the world over have formed fighting organisations not necessarily because they were more grasping than other trades and professions, but because they had been used to dictating their terms of service and this practice had been challenged by consumers' representatives." (1)   Professor Eckstein commented: "The development of public sanitary and medical politics made the BMA more active in politics; but it had other effects on its role and power as well. First of all it has engendered a constant growth in the Association's membership since the mid nineteenth century......" (2)

In this respect the climate for mobilising collective action has been propitious. The BMA is typified as a "defensive" or "protective" association. Millerson (1964) refers to it as such, and Blackburn calls it, "one of the best known organisations of this type." (3)

If a situation where individuals are threatened is classed as propitious for such organisation one is left to carefully define "threat". Albert Breton (1974) argues that "coercion" leads to collective activity. He gives the example of such "coercion" stemming from government activity which does not conform with all individuals' preferences. More broadly, but in similar vein, Albert Hirschman (1970) distinguishes between individual action ('exit') and collective action ('voice'). Individual action is possible in a market which is competitive, where the individual may substitute between goods as prices change. In this way the market provides the "defensive mechanism" for individual action. Hirschman observes that: "Certain types of purchases may nevertheless lend themselves particularly to the voice option even though many buyers are involved. When the consumer has been dissatisfied with an inexpensive non-durable good he will most probably go over to a different variety without making a fuss. But if he is stuck with an expensive durable good such as an automobile which disappoints day in and day out he is less likely to remain silent." (4)

The market mechanism provides defence in the sense that when competition is evident the individual can substitute in the face of relative price changes. When markets do not function so as to protect the individual then he relies on non-market action. For example, commentators such as Milton Friedman (1962) have argued that the market mechanism can stand as a "safety valve" against the incompetence of government agencies. The case of education has been cited as one in which the private sector provides just such a role. It is the absence of the alternatives offered by a competitive market that leads individuals to feel that their only means of objecting to and contesting difficulties is by collective action and lobbying. Thus if a "threat" occurs individuals may respond collectively if individual action is thwarted.

The "threat" doctors may feel as a result of government action is that their current income level is at risk because of the monopsonistic position of the government.(5) If such is the case the individual cannot easily adjust to ensure that financial rate of return on the acquisition of his skills that he might have expected. The 'secure' income level that follows individual adjustment being considerably below the 'current' income level. He is stuck with a durable piece of human capital and the only action he can take in the light of potential disappointment is via collective action. The medical market offers the doctor little scope to individually attain his financial expectations. Both the existence of barriers to competition, in the form of a code of ethics, and the widespread coverage of the National Health Service reduces the ability of the doctor to respond individually to perceived "threats".

The extension of state medicine in 1911 found 40 per cent of the population of England and Wales covered by the NHI and 90 per cent of all general practitioners participating in it. (6) By July 1948 one estimate was that private practice shrank from being the normal form of medicine for over 50 per cent of the population to less than 4 per cent. (7) The private market has shrunk, while within the National Health Service remuneration has been based on a capitation fee. It has been widely observed that a capitation fee system of remuneration provides but a tenuous link between the work of a general practitioner and his reward. (8) The area in which the individual might feel that individual action could ensure an adequate financial return to his skills is therefore reduced. Everything has come to depend on the negotiating strength of the Association in setting capitation fees. To ensure, as far as is possible, the position he expects, the doctor must depend to a greater degree upon collective action.

The extension of government activity and the form in which it has developed constrains vigorous competition. Yet, of course, within the 'profession' such activity is to be frowned upon. However this is defended, the development of an ethical code has served to reduce competition among doctors. (9) Inevitably the emphasis has been thrown upon collective rather than individual action.

That doctors may feel threatened as a group is not surprising. To the extent that the politician is viewed as a vote maximiser the doctor may feel his interests are likely to be sacrificed to those of the consumer and the taxpayer. (10) The provision of better public services at a lower cost may prove a popular political platform but may not conform to a bolstering of the income of doctors. (11) Indeed as Buchanan (1965) points out, the structure of the National Health Service is such that financial inadequacies are predictable. To the extent that no price is charged for the services of doctors, demand will increase. However, inasmuch as revenue is raised via taxation, individuals prefer to keep as low as possible their tax payments. The result will be pressure on those involved within the health service; pressure reflected in insufficient resources for the demand placed upon them and the consequent growth of waiting lists.

As far as evidence is concerned, Alan Maynard (1975) has recently compared the forms of medical care provision in the countries of the EEC. The original six members of the EEC experienced much less government intervention in their medical markets, the expenditure on medical care has grown faster in those countries than in the UK. This however did not appear to signify that the quality and quantity of medical care is superior. As such it may be considered to reflect the lack of opposition to the medical profession which in the UK is found in the existence of the monopsonistic powers of the DHSS.

If doctors in this way feel "threatened" their position is all the more vulnerable given the specific nature of their skills. As Link and London (1975) comment, "The clearest evidence of an association between depressed wage levels and monopsony is found in markets where specialised skills are required and close alternative occupations are few." (12) If doctors fear such a situation then their current income level may not be regarded as secure. As the growth of this "threat" develops, the secure level of income that doctors may regard as maintained by individual action in the market is well below the current level of income. It has been shown that though doctors may feel their contribution to an association has little chance of proving significant they are more inclined to take the gamble in such a situation. As is apparent, to pursue any alternative individual action is likely to prove abortive. Contribution to collective action is the only real alternative and the inclination to contribute will grow as a "threat" is felt.

The Association of course can only benefit from such a situation. Though the association battles for their members it is clearly advantageous that the "threat" remains possible. The BMA, as an association, in this way benefits from both the growth of the government's role and the extension of the constraints of medical ethics. That sub-sets within the profession can believe themselves threatened by comparison with each other would signify an environment in which political entrepreneurship will thrive; hence the JHDA and HCSA.

8.2   FINAL COMMENTS

This case study has inevitably drawn consideration of two distinct questions. Firstly, with respect to the BMA itself and secondly, with respect to the analysis of collective action. To illustrate with reference to the former, it is possible to present an interesting case that the BMA as an association has benefited by the involvement of government in the medical market. Public agencies were generally easier to deal with than the private institutions of the nineteenth century. Indeed the BMA was welcomed into a partnership in the administration of a national health service. Prestige and political expertise were acquired in negotiations. Negotiations which created uncertainty in the minds of doctors who rallied to their spokesman. Ironically it would appear that the BMA has never required

158

quite the coercive authority over the profession that has been revealed by associations in more market orientated environments. If problems were to arise, they would appear in representing ever more distinct sections of the profession in negotiation with a common paymaster.

While such aspects of the life of the BMA invite consideration in and of themselves, the study offers observations on the analysis of collective behaviour. Closed shop authority and selective private incentives did not in and of themselves adequately explain membership. While private inducements could not be completely discounted, they were better considered as ways in which the costs of membership, and of the gamble involved, were reduced by the organisation. In this way they are compatible with the changes in the environment that increase demand for membership. Both factors lead to an increase in collective action, if it is considered that individuals feel that the expected value of contribution is not certainly zero. The entrepreneurship and organisation which associations provide is the catalyst which brings about collective action. In this study the existence of an association offering an array of private inducements has proved the focus for individuals responding to what might be viewed as a threat situation. Though not pursued in this study, it is clearly the case that there may be an optimum amount of selective incentives given the environment. A trade off may be evident for some associations, e.g. greater emphasis on private inducements as the group becomes more heterogeneous or as it feels no significant threat.

Political entrepreneurship offers itself as an obvious bridge between the approaches to collective behaviour. It is an area in which more research is required. For example, will direct contact by an organisation alter the individual's perceptions as to the value of his contribution? In this study, evidence in chapter three would seem to suggest this view. Similarly in quite different case studies, this aspect of entrepreneurship is considered important. For example, Bruce Bolnick examined participation in self help projects of community development in Kenya. "Willing" contribution increased following communication between leaders and participants at rallies. Similarly Kikuchi, Dozina and Hayami, looking at voluntary community development in the Philippines commented, "unless there had been good leaders in the community .... such a project would not have materialised." (13)

Much attention has been drawn to the costs of political activity, such as voting or joining associations. Barry (1970) has raised the argument that such costs are typically not great. It might be argued that there is a "threshold" above which costs and returns influence a person's actions and below which they do not. Thus, if a positive action is needed to join associations (e.g. sending off money, getting in touch with organisation officials) then

159

membership will be low. On the other hand, if effort is required to avoid membership then inertia will operate the other way. In keeping with this argument Butler and Stokes (1969) found in their surveys a substantial proportion of individuals who would have joined unions had they only been asked. To such an extent active political entrepreneurs will be able to operate. If substantial numbers within the group join associations then others may follow suit in the belief that their predecessors undertook the decision costs and chose correctly. In such a fashion entrepreneurs gain from "tradition" or "custom".

Strategies of political entrepreneurs ought also to be related to their objectives. In much the same way as the theory of the firm has been related to alternative goals of management and the theory of public expenditure has been developed with reference to the objectives of bureaucrats, the analysis of collective action should be related to the interests of leadership. (14) When profit is maximised one could envisage output of the association determined where aggregate marginal revenue equals the aggregate of marginal costs of provision of the good and of the collection organisation. In cases where their prestige is linked to output and is the objective to be maximised it is conceivable that total output may be in excess of this output. The degree of competition will also be an important feature in analysing the entrepreneur's role in the provision of collective goods.

That the environment in which entrepreneurship operates is significant is quite clear. The intervention of government in the lives of workers of many different backgrounds appear to have produced the same result. (15) It is of interest in this respect to note that in a recent survey by Gennard, Dunn and Wright (1980), areas of high union density with little or no demand for the closed shop include two million workers such as high grade civil servants, teachers in primary, secondary and higher education, post office engineers and management grades in the post office and health service. This full complement of examples, which they list, are clearly labour markets affected by the intervention of government. There are of course many other areas where the uncertainty invoked by government involvement has led to collective action. E.g. Self and Storing (1962) note the growth of the National Farmer's Union in the UK in the light of the falling importance of the squire in Parliament and the growth of government concern with agriculture. In examining trade associations, close analysis of the CBI identified government proposals for nationalisation as a motive for membership. (16)

As the possibility is accepted that in certain situations entrepreneurship can engender the organisation for collective action, then the case for closed shop powers becomes less naive. Recently Bennett and Johnson (1979)

comment that the existence of the closed shop based on the
free-rider problem is open to question. Indeed they
suggest "that the free rider is more of an artifice of the
labour unions' own making than a major affliction." (17)
Union leadership may find their tasks easier and possibly
the scope to pursue their own objectives wider with such
closed shop power. The forced rider becomes as relevant
as the free-rider. What is clear is that the free-rider
problem cannot automatically be held up as a case for such
authority. (18) The appropriate comparison is that of the
outcomes with and without such authority before assessment
can be made of its desirability.

This study then directs us to consider the role of
leadership and the environment in which it stands. The
free-rider problem in the strictest form predicts no
voluntary contribution towards collective goods. In some
circumstances this may apply but there may be a wide range
of cases in which political entrepreneurs can mobilise some
collective action.

NOTES

1   B. Abel-Smith (1963) p.34
2   H. Eckstein (1960) p.44
3   R.M. Blackburn (1967) p.26
4   A.C. Hirschman (1970) p.42
5   The current income levels of doctors may not of course
    accord to the rumuneration of a competitive market
6   R. Stevens (1966) p.53
7   M.H. Cooper (1975) p.9
8   Professor Jewkes, Royal Commission on Doctors and
    Dentists Remuneration, (1960) Minority Report, para 74;
    Porritt (1962) para.196; D.S. Lees and M.H. Cooper
    (1963); W.A. Glasser (1970); E.J. Powell (1966);
    G. Forsythe (1966) all point to the discrepancy between
    work undertaken and remuneration to the doctors.
9   An example may be seen in D.T.C. Barlow (1973),
    "Whilst a little friendly competition amongst
    colleagues can do no harm, head hunting is to be
    strongly deprecated."
10 R.E. Wagner (1966) points out that large groups do not
    necessarily organise themselves because they have
    influence directly on the legislature. In large
    number groups directly affect vote maximising
    politicians and hence do not require formal
    associations.
11 For example, note that an attitude survey in the
    Review Body on Top Salaries First Report, Cmnd 4836
    HMSO 1971, showed that the public believed the
    "appropriate" salary for a GP was £4,100 per annum
    which was less than they were earning at the time of
    the survey.
12 R. Link and J.H. London (1975) p.649
13 M. Kikuchi, G. Dozina and Y. Hayami (1978) p.213
14 See for example R. Morris (1967) and W.A. Niskanen (1973)

15   See, for example, W.E. Steslicke (1973) whose
      membership figures for the Japan Medical Association
      show a growth at the time that a national insurance
      scheme was implemented. In the UK the birth of the
      National Union of Teachers can be traced to 1870, the
      year the government took greater responsibility for
      primary education (see N. Morris (1969)). More
      recently the growth of the National Federation of the
      Self Employed in the UK may be related to the
      introduction of value added tax.
16   See W. Grant (1979)
17   J.T. Bennett and M.H. Johnson (1979) p.170
18   The free-rider argument is not the sole rationale for
      closed shop powers. For example employers favour
      having one set of workers' representatives to deal
      with (see M. Hart (1979)).

Bibliography

Abel-Smith, B. "Paying the Family Doctor", Medical Care, Vol. 1, No. 1, January March, 1963, pp 27-35.

Abel-Smith, B. The Hospitals 1800-1948: A Study in Social Administration in England and Wales, Heineman, London 1964

Abel-Smith, B and Gales, K. British Doctors at Home and Abroad, Occasional Papers on Social Administration,Welwyn, Codicote Press for the Social Administration Trust, 1964.

Almond, G.A. and Verba, S. The Civic Culture, Little and Brown, Beaton, 1965.

Arrow, K.J. Social Choice and Individual Values, Yale University, London-New Haven, 1951.

Ashenfelter, G. and Pencavel, J.A. "Americal Trade Union Growth 1900-1960", Quarterly Journal of Economics, Vol. 83, August, 1969.

Bacharach, M. Economics and the Theory of Games, Macmillan, London, 1976.

Bain, G.S. The Growth of White Collar Unionism, Clarendon Press, Oxford, 1970.

Bain, G.S. and Elsheikh Farouk, "An Inter-industry Analysis of Unionisation in Britain", British Journal of Industrial Relations, Vol. XVIII, No. 2, July 1979, pp 137-157.

Bakke, E. Wight, "Why workers join unions", Personnel, July, 1945, Vol. 22, No. 1

Barlow, D.J.C., British General Practice, London, 1973.

Barry, Brian M. Sociologists, Economists and Democracy, Macmillan Collier, London, 1970.

Barzel, Y. and Silberberg, E. "Is the Act of Voting Rational", Public Choice, Vol. XVI, Fall 1973, pp 51-58.

Baumol, W.J. Business Behaviour, Value and Growth, Macmillan, New York, 1959.

Baumol, W.J. Welfare Economics and the Theory of the State, London, 1965.

Baumol, W.J. Economic Theory and Operations Analysis Prentice Hall, New Jersey, 1977, fourth edition.

Bennett, J.T. and Johnson, M.H. "Free Riders in US Labour Unions Artiface or Affliction", British Journal of Industrial Relations, Vol. XVIII, No. 2, July 1979, pp 158-173.

Bernstein, I. "The Growth of American Unions", American Economic Review, Vol. LXL, 1964.

Blackburn, R.M. Union Character and Social Class, London 1967.

Blondel, J. Voters, Parties and Leaders, Penguin, Harmondsworth, 1967.

Bloom, Howard S. and Douglas Price, H. "Voter Response to Short run Economic Conditions: The Asymmetric Effect of Poverty and Depression", American Journal of Political Science, December, 1975.

Blum, A.A. "Why Unions Grow", Labor History, 1968.

Blum, A.A. Teachers Unions and Associations: A comparative Study, Unwin, Illinois Press, Urbana, 1969.

Bohm, P. "An approach to the problem of estimating the demand for public goods", Swedish Journal of Economics, Vol. 73, 1971, pp 55-66.

Bohm, P. "Estimating Demand for Public Goods: An Experiment" European Economic Review, Vol. 3, 1972, pp 111-30.

Bolnick, B. "Collective Goods Provision through Community Development", Economic Development and Cultural Change Vol. 25, pp 137-50.

Boulding, K. "Economics as a Moral Science", American Economic Review, 1969, pp 1-12.

Brand, J.L. "The Parish Doctor: England's Poor Law Medical Officers and Medical Reform", Bulletin of the History of Medicine, Vol. 25, 1961.

Brand, J.L. Doctors and the State: The British Medical Profession and Government Action in Public Health 1870-1912, John Hopkins Press, Baltimore, 1965.

Bray, J. Dyer. The Doctors and the Insurance Act: A Statement of the Medical Man's Case against the Act. Manchester, 1912.

Breton, A. and Breton, R. "An economic theory of Social movements", American Economic Review, 59,1969, pp 198-205.

Breton, A. The Economic Theory of Representative Government, Aldine, Chicago, 1974.

Brockbank, C.M. The Foundation of Provincial Medical Education, Manchester University Press, 1936.

Brown, C.V. and Jackson, P.M. Public Sector Economics Martin Robertson, Oxford, 1978.

Brown, R.G.S. The Management of Welfare, Fontana, Glasgow, 1975.

Buchanan, J.M. "Politics, Policy and Pigovian Margins", Economica, 1962.

Buchanan, J.M. and Stubblebine W."Externality", Economica November, 1962.

Buchanan, J.M. The Inconsistencies of the National Health Service, Institute of Economic Affairs, London, 1965.

Buchanan, J.M. "An economic theory of clubs", Economica, 1965, pp 1-14.

Buchanan, J.M. "Ethical Rules, expected values and large numbers", Ethics, Vol. LXXCI, No.1, October, 1965.

Buchanan, J.M. "Co-operation and conflict in Public Goods Interaction, Western Economic Journal, March, 1967.

Buchanan, J.M. The Demand and Supply of Public Goods, Rand McNally & Co., Chicago, 1968.

Buchanan, J.M. and Tullock, G. The Calculus of Consent, Ann Arbor, University of Michigan, 1969.

Burkhead, J. and Miner, J. Public Expenditure, Macmillan, 1971.

Burton, John. "Are Trade Unions a Public Good/Bad? The Economics of the Closed Shop in Public Goods or Public Bads." E.A. Trade Unions Readings 17, pp 42-52, London 1978.

Butler, D. and Stokes, D. Political Change in Britain, Penguin, Harmondsworth, 1969.

Carr-Saunders, A.M. and Wilson, P.A. The Professions, Oxford, 1933.

Castles, F.G. _Pressure Groups and Political Culture_,
Routledge and Kegan Paul, London, 1967.

Chaffen, L. "The Psychological Effects of Unionism on the
Member", _Journal of Social Psychology_, 1947, 25, pp 133-37

Chamberlain, N.W. "Review of M. Olson, Jr., The Logic of
Collective Action", _American Economic Review_, 1966.

Chamberlin, J. "Provision of Collective Goods as a Function
of Group Size", _Americal Political Science Review_,
Vol. 68, 1974.

Chamberlin, J. Review of Frohlich et al. _Public Choice_
1973, pp 127-129.

Clarke, Edward, H. "Multipart Pricing of Public Goods
Public Choice, Vol. 11, 1971, pp 17-33.

Clark, Sir. G. _The Royal College of Physicians of London_
Vol, 11, Clarendon Press, Oxford, 1966.

Clegg, H.A. _The System of Industrial Relations in Great
Britain_, Basil Blackwell, Oxford, 1970.

Coase, R.H. "The Lighthouse in Economics", _Journal of Law
and Economics_, Vol. 7, 1974, pp 357-76.

Cole, G.D.H. _Studies in Class Structure_, London, 1955.

Coleman, J.S. "Individual Interest and Collective Action",
Papers on Non Market Decision Making, 1966.

Collard, D. _Altruism and Economy: A Study in Non Selfish
Economics_, Martin Robertson, Oxford, 1978.

Collings, J.S. "General Practice in England Today",
The Lancet, 25 March, 1950.

Colm, G. "Comment on Samuelson's theory of Public Finance",
Review of Economics and Statistics, November, 1956.

Conybeare, Sir J. "The Crises of 1911-13", _The Lancet_
May 18, 1957.

Cooper, M.A. _Rationing Health Care_, Croom Helm, London,
1975.

Cooper, M.H. and Culyer, A.J. "An Economic Survey of the
Nature and Intent of the British National Health Service"
Social Service and Medicine, Vol.5, No. 1, 1971.

Cowan, D.L. "Liberty, Laissez-faire and Licensure in
Nineteenth Century Britain", _Bulletin of the History of
Medicine_, Vol. 43, 1969, p.33

Cox, Alfred. _Among the Doctors_, Christopher Johnson,
London, 1950.

Culyer, A.J. "The Nature of the Commodity 'health care'
and its efficient allocation" _Oxford Economic Papers_
Vol. 23, 1971, pp 189-211.

Culyer, A.J. "The Economics of Health" in _Current Issues
in Economic Policy_, edited by R.W. Grant and G.K. Shaw
Current Issues in Economic Policy, Philip Allan, Oxford,
1975.

Daly, E. and Gierts, F. "Benevolence, Malevolence and
Economic Theory", _Public Choice_, 1972, Vol. XIII,
pp 1-20.

Davis, H.B. "The Theory of Union Growth", _Quarterly
Journal of Economics_, Vol. 55, 1941, pp 611-33.

Donnan, S.P.D. "British Medical Undergraduates in 1975:
a student survey in 1975 compared with 1966" _Medical
Education_, Vol.10, 1976, pp 341-7.

Dopson, L. _The Changing Scene in General Practice_, London,
1971.

Douglas-Wilson, I. and McLachlon, G. Health Service Prospects: An International Survey, The Lancet and Nuffield Provincial Hospitals Trust, London, 1973.

Downs, A. An Economic Theory of Democracy, Harper & Row, New York, 1957.

Dvorak, E.J. "Will engineers unionise?" Industrial Relations, Vol. 2, 1962-3.

Earwicker, Ray. "A Study of the BMA-TUC Joint Committee on Medical Questions 1935-1939", Journal of Social Policy, Vol. 8, Part 3, 1979, pp 335-356.

Eckstein, Harry H. The English Health Service, Oxford University Press, London, 1959.

Eckstein, Harry H. Pressure Group Politics: the case of the British Medical Association, George Allen and Unwin, London, 1960.

Elliot, P. The Sociology of the Professions, MacMillan, London, 1972.

Elston, Mary Ann. "Medical Autonomy: Challenge and Response" in K. Barnard and K. Lee, Conflicts in the National Health Service, Croom Helm, London, 1977.

Escarrez, D.R. The Price Theory of Value in Public Finance, University of Florida Press, Gainesville, Florida, 1966.

Evans, A.W. "Private Goods Externality Public Good" Scottish Journal of Political Economy, February, 1970.

Ferejohn, John A. and Fiorina, Morris P. "The Paradox of not Voting: A Decision Theoretic Analysis, The American Political Science Review, Vol. 68, 1974, pp 525-536.

Ferris, P. The Doctors, Penguin, Harmondsworth, 1971.

Finer, S.E. Anonymous Empire: A study of the Lobby in Great Britain, Pall Mall, London, 1969.

Forbes, R. Sixty Years of Medical Defence, The Medical Defence Union Ltd. London, 1948.

Forsythe, G. Doctors and State Medicine, Pitman Medical, London, 1966.

Friedman, M. and Savage, L.J. "The Utility Analysis of Choice Involving Risks", Journal of Political Economy, 1948.

Friedman, M. and Kusnets, S. Income from Independent Professional Practice, New York National Bureau of Economic Research, 1954.

Friedman, M. Capitalism and Freedom, University of Chicago Press, Chicago, 1962.

Frohlich, N. and Oppenheimer, J. "I get by with a little help from my friends", World Politics, 23 October 1970 pp 104-120.

Frohlich, N. Oppenheimer, J.A. and Young, O.R. Political Leadership and Collective Goods, Princeton University Press, New Jersey, 1971.

Fuchs, V.R. (ed) Production and Productivity in the Service Industries. NBER. New York, 1969.

Garceau, O. The Political Life of the AMA, Harvard University Press, Mass. 1941.

Gennard, John. Dunn, Stephen and Wright, Michael. "The extent of closed shop arrangements in British industry" Employment Gazette, January 1980. pp 16-22.

Gilbert, B.B. The Evolution of National Insurance in Great Britain, Michael Joseph, London, 1966.

Gish, O. Doctor Migration and World Health, Occasional
papers on Social Admin. No.43, G. Bell and Sons, 1971.
Glass, D.V. (ed) Social Mobility in Britain, London, 1953.
Glasser, W.A. Paying the Doctor. John Hopkins Press,
Baltimore, 1970.
Goldin, K.D. "Equal Access vs. Selective Access: A
Critique of Public Goods Theory" Public Choice, 1977,
pp 53-71.
Gosden, P.H.J.H. The Friendly Societies in England 1815-
1875. Manchester, 1961. Manchester University Press
Graham, J. "What professional people earn". The Scotsman,
13 February 1965.
Grant, W. and Marsh, D. The CBI. Hodder and Stoughton,
London, 1977.
Grant, W. "On joining Interest Groups: A comment"
British Journal of Political Science, Vol. 9, Part I,
1979, pp 126-128.
Hardin, R. "Collective Action as an Agreeable N-
PPrisoner's Dilemma" Behavioural Science, Vol. 16, 1971
pp 472-281.
Hardy, H.N. The State of the Medical Profession in Great
Britain and Ireland in 1900. Fannin, Dublin, 1901.
Harris, R. (ed) Freedom-for-All, Institute of Economic
Affairs, London, 1865.
Hart, Moira. "Why bosses love the closed shop",
New Society. 15 February 1979.
Hausknecht, M. The Joiners, Bedminster Press, New York,
1962.
Head, J.G. "Public Goods and Public Policy", Public
Finance, 1962.
Head, J.G. "The theory of public goods", Rivista Di
Diritte Finanziario E Scienza Della Finanze, Giveno,
1968, Anno XXVII, No. 2.
Health, The Open University, London, 1972.
Herber, J.M. Britain and Health, Penguin, 1939.
Hill, C. and Woodcock, J. The National Health Service
Christopher Johnson, London, 1949.
Hill, K.R. "Medical education at the crossroads" BMJ
Vol. 1, 1966, pp 970-973.
Hindell, K. Trade Union Membership, Political and Economic
Planning, London, 1962.
Hines, A.G. "Trade Unions and Wage Inflation in the
United Kingdom: 1893-1961. Review of Economic Studies
Vol. 31, 1964.
Hirshman, A.O. Exit, Voice and Loyalty, Harvard University
Press, Cambridge, Mass. 1970.
Hochman, H.H. and Rodgers, J.D. "Pareto Optimal
Redistribution", American Economic Review, Vol.59, 1969.
Hodgkinson, R. The Origins of the NHS, Wellcome Historical
Medical Library, London, 1967.
Hogarth, J. Payment of the General Practitioner, Pergamon
Press, London, 1963.
Holloway, S.W.F. The British Medical Association 1832-83'
(unpublished).
Holloway, S.W.F. "Medical Education in England 1830-58"
"History" XLIX, (167) 1964.

Honigsbaum, F. The Struggle for the Ministry of Health,
   Occasional Papers on Social Administration, No.37, 1970.
   Willmer Bros. Ltd., Burkenhead.
Hughes, J. Patterns of Trade Union Growth, TU Research
   Unit, Ruskin College, Oxford.
Hyde, D.R. and Wolff, P. "The American Medical Association:
   Power, Purpose and Politics in Organised Medicine",
   The Yale Law Journal, Vol.63, No.7, 1954, pp 938-1002.
Ireland, T.R. "The Calculus of Philanthropy", Public
   Choice, Vol. VII, Fall 1969, pp 23-31.

Jewkes, J and S. The Genesis of the British National
   Service, Basil Blackwell, Oxford, 1962.
Johansen, L. "The theory of public goods: misplaced
   emphasis? Journal of Public Economics, Vol. 7, 1977,
   pp 147-152.
Johnson, T.J. Professions and Power, Macmillan, London,
   1972.
Jones, P.R. "Why Doctors Join the British Medical
   Association", Social and Economic Administration, Vol.7
   No.3, 1973.
Jones, P.R. "The British Medical Association and the
   Closed Shop", Industrial Relations Journal, Winter,
   Vol.4, No.4, 1974.
Jones, P.R. "The Growth of the British Medical Association:
   A Case Study in Collective Behaviour", Social and
   Economic Administration, Vol.12, No.1, Spring 1978,
   pp 36-45.
Jones, P.R. "The Appeal of the Political Entrepreneur"
   British Journal of Political Science, Vol.8, part 4,
   October, 1978.
Kassalow, E.M. "White Collar Unionism in Western Europe"
   Monthly Labor Review, LXXXVI, 1963.
Keating, B. "The Characteristics and Survival of Public
   Interest Groups", Atlantic Economic Review, Vol. 3,
   December, 1977, pp 42-49.
Keating, B. "Economics of Pressure Group Influence: Among
   the 'Political Entrepreneur '", Antitrust Law and
   Economics Review, Vol.10, 1978, pp 93-101.
Kelsall, R.K. Report on an Inquiry into Application for
   Admission to the Universities, 1957.
Kessel, R.A. "Price Discrimination in Medicine", Journal
   of Law and Economics, October 1958, pp 20-53.
Kessel, R.A. "The AMA and the Supply of Physicians",
   Law and Contemporary Problems, Spring, 1970, No.2,
   Vol, XXXV.
Key, V.O. Politics, Parties, Pressure Groups, 4th edition
   Thomas Y Cromwell, New York, 1958, p143.
Kikuchi, M. Dozina, G. and Hayami, Y. "Economics of
   Community Work Programs: A Communal Irrigation Project
   In the Philippines", Economic Development and Cultural
   Change, Vol.26, 1978, pp 211-25.
Klein, R. Complaints against Doctors: A Study in
   Professional Accountability, Charles Knight & Co. 1973,
   London.
Klein, R. "National Health Service after Re-organisation",
   Political Quarterly, 1973, Vol.44.

Klein, R. "Policy Making in the National Health Service" _Political Studies_, Vol. 22, 1974, pp 1-14.

Klein, R. "Reports and Surveys", The Profession of Medicine, _The Political Quarterly_, Vol. 46, No. 3 July-August, 1975. pp 338-340.

Laver, R.J. and Rees, M. _Problems and Progress in Medical Care_, 7th series, 1972. Nuffield Provincial Hospital Trust, OUP.

Lees, D.S. and Cooper, M.H. "The Capitation Fee", _The Lancet_, 20 April, 1963. (a)

Lees, D.S. and Cooper, M.H. "The Work of the General Practitioner", _The Journal of the College of General Practitioners_, Vol. 6, 1963 (b)

Lees, D.S. _Economic Consequences of the Professions_, Institute of Economic Affairs, London, 1966.

Lincoln, J.A. _Journey to Coercion: from Tolpuddle to Rookes v Barnard_. IEA. London, 1964

Lindsey, A. _Socialised Medicine in England and Wales_, The National Health Service, London, Oxford University Press, 1962

Link, R. and London, J.H. "Monoposony and Union Power in the market for Nurses", _Southern Economic Journal_, April, 1975, pp 649-659.

Little, E.M. _History of the British Medical Association 1832-1932_. London BMA

Litvack, James M. and Oates, Wallace E. "Group size and the Output of Public Goods: Theory and an Application to State-Local Finance in the United States", _Public Finance_ Vol. 25, 1970, pp 42-58.

Lockwood, D.T. _The Black Coated Worker_, Unwin, London, 1966

Logan, W.P.D. and Cashion, A.A. Studies on Medical and Population Subjects, 1958.

London and Provincial Directory 1847

Loveridge, R. _Collective Bargaining by National Employees in the United Kingdom_, Ann Arbor, 1971.

Machlachlan, F. (ed) _Problems and Progress in Medical Care_ 7th series, OUP, 1972

MacIver, R.M. and Page, C.H. _Society: An Introductory Analysis_, Rinehart, New York, 1959.

Mapother, E.D. _The Medical Profession_, Fannin and Co. Dublin, 1968.

Margolis, J. "A comment of the pure theory of public expenditure", _Review of Economics and Statistics_, Vol. 37, 1954.

Margolis, J. _The Public Economy of Urban Communities_ John Hopkins Press, Baltimore, 1965.

Margolis, J. and Guitton, H. (eds) _Public Economics_, Macmillan Collier, London, 1969.

Marglin, S.A. "The Social rate of discount and the Optimal rate of Investment", _Quarterly Journal of Economics_ February, 1963.

Marmor, T.R. and Thomas, D. "Doctors, Politics and Pay Disputes: Pressure Group Politics Revisited" _British Journal of Political Science_, Vol.2, 1972, p 432.

Marris, R. _The Economic Theory of 'Managerial' Capitalism_, Macmillan, London, 1964.

Marsh, D. "On Joining Interest Groups: An Empirical
  Consideration of the Work of Mancur Olson Jr."
  British Journal of Political Science, Vol.6, pp 257-271.
Marsh, D. "More on Joining Interest Groups", British
  Journal of Political Science, Vol. 8, 1978, pp 380-384.
Maynard, A. Health Care in the European Community,
  Croom Helm, London, 1975.
Maynard, A. "Medical Care in the European Community",
  New Society, 28 August, 1975.
McCarthy, W.E.J. The Closed Shop in Britain, Basil
  Blackwell, Oxford, 1964.
McKersie R.B. and Brown, M. "Non professional Hospital
  Workers and a Union Organising Drive", Quarterly Journal
  of Economics, Vol. 76, August, 1963.
McMenemey, W.H. The Life and Times of Sir Charles Hastings,
  Edinburgh, London.
McMillan, J. "The Free Rider Problem: A Survey",
  The Economic Record, Vol.55, No.149, 1979, pp 95-107.
Mechanic, D. and Faich, R.G. "Doctors in Revolt, The Crisis
  in the English NHS". Medical Care, Vol. 8, 1970.
Mell, W. "Basic Journal List for Small Hospital Libraries"
  Bulletin of the Medical Library Association, July 1969,
  Vol. 57, No.3
Mencher, A. Private Practice in Britain, Occasional Papers
  on Social Administration, No.24, London, ·1967.
Merskey, H. "Some Features of Medical Education in Great
  Britain during the first half of the Nineteenth Century"
  British Journal of Medical Education, 1969.
Millerson, G. The Qualifying Association: A Study in
  Professionalisation, Routledge and Kegan Paul, London
  1964.
Millward, R. Public Expenditure Economics, McGraw Hill,
  London, 1971.
Mishan, E.J. "The Relationship between Joint Products,
  Collective Goods and External Effects", Journal of
  Political Economy, 1969, pp 329-428.
Mishan, E.J. "The post war literature on externalities"
  Journal of Economic Literature, 1971.
The Modern Hospital, Vol. 103, July 1964.
Morland, S.T. "Olson's Logic of Collective Action: A
  Review article", Review of Social Economy, March, 1967,
  Vol. XXV, No.1
Morris, N. "England" in Teachers Unions and Associations:
  A comparative study, University of Illinois Press
  Urbana, 1969.
Morton, J. "Women Doctors", New Society, 28 February 1974
Musgrave, R.A. The Theory of Public Finance, McGraw Hill,
  London, 1959.
Musgrave, R.A. and Peacock, A.T. Classics in the Theory
  of Public Finance, Macmillan, 1967.
Musgrave, R.A. Fiscal Systems, Yale University Press,
  New Haven - London, 1969.
Newman, C. The Evolution of Medical Education in the 19th·
  Century, London, Oxford University Press, 1957.
Newsholme, Sir A. Medicine and the State, London, 1932

Newsholme, Sir A. The Last Thirty Years in Public Health, George Allen and Unwin, London, 1936, p.368.

Ng, Yew Kwang, "The Economic Theory of Clubs: Pareto Optimality Conditions" Economica, 1973.

Niskanen, W.A. Bureaucracy: Servant or Master, Institute of Economic Affairs, London, 1973.

Office of Health Economics, The Consumer and the Health Service, London, 1968.

Olson, M. Jr. and MacFarland, D. "The Restoration of Pure Monopoly and the Concept of the Industry", Quarterly Journal of Economics, November, 1962.

Olson, M. Jr and Zeckhauser, R. "An Economic Theory of Alliances", Review of Economics and Statistics, August 1966, pp 266-279.

Olson, M. Jr. and Zeckhauser, R. "Collective Goods, Comparative Advantage and Alliance Efficiency", in McKean, R.N. (ed) Issues in Defense Economics, National Bureau of Economic Research, Columbia University Press, New York, 1967.

Olson, M. Jr. The Logic of Collective Action, New York, 1968.

Olson, M. Jr. "Economics, Sociology and the best of all possible worlds", The Public Interest, No.12, Summer, 1968.

Page, D. and Jones, K. Health and Welfare Services in Britain in 1978. Occasional Paper No. XXII. National Institute of Economic and Social Research, Cambridge University Press.

Parry, N. and Parry, J. The Rise of the Medical Profession Croom Helm, London, 1976.

Parsons, M.B. Perspectives in the Study of Politics, Rand McNally and Co. Chicago, Illinois, 1968.

Parsons, T. Essays in Sociological Theory, Glencoe, Illinois, 1954.

Pauly, M.V. "Clubs, Commonality and the Core: An integration of game theory and the theory of public goods" Economica, August, 1967.

Pauly, M.V. "Optimality, 'Public' Goods and Local Governments: A General Theoretical Analysis", Journal of Political Economy, LXXVII, 1970, pp 572-585.

Peacock, A.T. and Wiseman, J. The Growth of Public Expenditure in the United Kingdom, National Bureau of Economic Research, Princeton University Press, Princeton, 1961.

Peacock, A.T. The Economic Analysis of Government, Martin Robertson, London, 1979.

Pencavel, J.H. "The Demand for Union Services: An Exercise" Industrial and Labour Relations Journal, Vol. 24, 1970-71, pp 180-190.

Pendrill, G.R. Surveys on the Use of Periodicals in some British Medical Libraries. University of Sheffield Postgraduate School of Librarianship.

Penrose, L.S. "Elementary Statistics of Majority Voting" Journal of the Royal Statistical Society, Vol. 109, 1946.

Peston, M. Public Goods and the Public Sector, Macmillan, 1972.

Potter, A. Organised Groups in British Politics, Faber,
London, 1961.
Powell, J.E. A New Look at Medicine and Politics,
Pitman, London Medical Publishing Co. Ltd. 1966.
Poynter, F.N.L. (ed) The Evolution of Medical Education in
Britain, Pitman, London, 1966.
Prandy, K. "Professional Organisation in Great Britain"
Industrial Relations, Vol.V. October, 1965. pp 67-69.
Raising, L.M. "World Biomedical Journals 1951-60"
Bulletin of the Medical Library Association, April 1966
Vol.54, No.2
Rapoport, A. and Chammah, A.M. Prisoner's Dilemma,
University of Michigan Press, 1965.
Rayack, E. Professional Power and American Medicine: The
Economics of the AMA. World Publishing Co. New York,
1967.
Rees, A. The Economics of Trade Unions, Cambridge Universit
University Press, 1962.
Richelson, J. "A note on Collective Goods and the theory
of Political Entrepreneurship", Public Choice, 1972
pp 73-75.
Ricketts, M. "Is 'Efficiency' more Important than Justice
and 'Equity'", IEA Readings 17, IEA London 1978 pp 53-54
Rikker, W.H. The Theory of Political Coalition, New Haven
Yale University Press, 1962.
Rikker, W.H. and Ordeshook, O.C. "A Theory of the Calculus
of Voting", American Political Science Review, Vol. 62,
1968, pp 25-42.
Rivington, W. The Medical Profession of the United Kingdom'
Fannin & Co. Dublin, 1883.
Roberts, B.C. Trade Union Government and Administration in
Great Britain, Bell, London, 1956.
Roberts, B.C. Trade Unions in a Free Society, 2nd ed.
London Institute of Economic Affairs, 1962.
Roberts, B.C. (ed) Industrial Relations:Contemporary
Problems and Perspectives, Methuen, London, 1962.
Robson, J. "The NHS Company Inc? The Social Consequences
of the Professional Dominance in the NHS". International
Journal of Health Services, Vol.3, 1973, pp 413-23.
Rolleston, Sir A. "Medical Friendships, Clubs and Societ
Societies", Annals of Medical History, Vol.XI, May,1930.
Routh, G. "Future Trade Union Membership", in Industrial
Relations Contemporary Problems and Perspectives,
edited by Roberts, B.C. Methuen, London, 1962.
Routh, G. Occupation and Pay in Great Britain 1906-60.
Cambridge University Press, Cambridge, 1965.
Rowan, R.L. and Northrup, H.R. Readings in Labor Economics
and Labor Relations, Irwin, Illinois, 1968.
Salisbury, R.H. "An exchange theory of interest groups"
Midwest Journal of Political Science, Vol.13, 1969,
pp 1-32.
Samuelson, P.A. "Diagrammatic Exposition of a Theory of
Public Expenditure", Review of Economics and Statistics'
Vol. 37, 1953.
Samuelson, P.A. "The Pure Theory of Public Expenditure",
Review of Economics and Statistics, Vol.36, 1954,
pp 387-9.

Samuelson, P.A. "Contrast between welfare conditions for
   joint supply and for public goods", Review of Economics
   and Statistics, February, 1969.
Scitovsky, T. Welfare and Competition, George Allen and
   Unwin, London, 1966.
Seidman, J., London, J. and Karsh, B. "Why workers join
   unions" Annals of American Academy of Political and
   Social Sciences, 1951, pp 75-84.
Self, P.J.O. and Storing, H.J. The State and the Farmer
   Allen and Unwin, London, 1962.
Shackleton, J.R. "Dr. Marsh on Olson: A comment"
   British Journal of Political Science, Vol. 8, 1978,
   pp 375-380.
Shapiro, D.L. "Pressure Groups and Public Investment
   Decisions" Public Choice, Spring 1971, Vol.X pp 103-108
Sharp, A.M. and Escarraz, D.R. "A reconsideration of the
   Price or Exchange theory of public finance", Southern
   Economic Journal, October 1964, pp 132-39.
Shaw, Batty A. "The Oldest medical societies in Great
   Britain", Medical History, Vol.XIII, 1968.
Shister, J. "The Logic of Union Growth" Journal of
   Political Economy, 1948.
Shoup, C.S. Public Finance, Chicago, 1969
Shumpeter, J. Capitalism, Socialism and Democracy, Harper
   and Row, New York, 1942.
Silberman, J. and Durdan, G. "The Rational Behaviour
   Theory of Voter Participation", Public Choice, Vol.XXIII,
   Fall, 1975.
Singer, C. and Holloway, S.W.F. "Early medical education
   in relation to the pre-history of London University",
   Medical History, Vol.4, 1960.
Smith, A. The Theory of Moral Sentiments, London, 1825.
Stacey, F. "The re-organisation of the National Health
   Service" Public Administration Bulletin, No.15
   December, 1973.
Steiner, P.O. The Economics of Public Finance, Brookings
   Institute, 1974
Stern, W. Britain Yesterday and Today. Longmans, London,
   1964.
Steslicke, W.E. Doctors in Politics: The Political Life
   of the Japan Medical Association. Praeger, London, 1973.
Stevens, R. Medical Practice in Modern England, New Haven
   and London, Yale University Press, 1966.
Stevens, R. American Medicine and the Public Interest,
   Yale University Press, New Haven and London, 1971.
Stigler, J. "Free Riders and Collective Action: An
   Appendix to theories of Economic Regulation" The Bell
   Journal of Economics and Management Science. Vol. 5,
   No. 2, Autumn, 1974.
Suranyi-Unger, T. "Individual and Collective Wants"
   The Journal of Political Economy, February 1948, Vol. LVI
   No. 1, pp 1-22.
Susser, N.W. and Watson, M. Sociology in Medicine, London
   Oxford University Press, 1962.
Tanzi, V. "A note on Exclusion, pure public goods and
   pareto optimality", Public Finance, 1972

Taylor, M. _Anarchy and Co-operation_, John Wiley and Sons London, 1976.

Thistlethwaite, R.A. "Doctors hold the key in Europe" _European Community_, No.12, December, 1973.

Thornton, J.L. _Medical Books, Libraries and Collectors_, London, 1949.

Tideman, T.N. and Tullock, G. "A new and superior process for making social choices", _Journal of Political Economy_ Vol. 84, 1976, pp 1145-1159.

Tiebout, C.M. "A pure theory of local expenditure" _Journal of Political Economy_, October, 1956.

Titmus, R.M. _Essays on 'The Welfare State'_ Unwin, University Books, London, 1963

Tollinson, R.D. "Consumption Sharing and Non-exclusion Rules" _Economica_, August, 1972, pp 276-291.

Trueman, D.B. _The Government Process_, Knopf, New York, 1951.

Tullock, G. "Information without Profit", _Papers on Non-Market Decision Making_, 1966

Tullock, G. _Private Wants, Public Means_, Basic Books, New York, 1970.

Turner, E.S. _Call the Doctor: A Social History of Medical Men_, New York, 1958.

Van der Vall, M. _Labor Organisations_, Cambridge University Press, 1970.

Vaughan, P. _Doctors Commons_, Heinemann, London, 1959.

Wagner, R. "Pressure groups and political entrepreneurs", _Papers on Non-Market Decision Making_, Journal 1, 1966.

Webb, S and B. _History of Trade Unionism, 1666-1920_ Longmans, London, 1920.

Weintraub, E. Roy, _Conflict and Co-operation in Economics_ Macmillan, London, 1975.

Wilensky, H. "The Professionalisation of Everyone?" _American Journal of Sociology_, Vol. LXIX, September, 1964.

Willcocks, A.J. _The Creation of the National Health Service_ Routledge and Kegan Paul, London, 1967.

Williams, A. "The Optimal Provision of Public Goods, in a system of Local Government", _Journal of Political Economy_, LXXIV, 1966, pp 18-33.

Wilson, C.W.M., Banks, J.A., Mapes, R.E.A. and Korte, S.M.T. "Influence of Different Sources of Therapeutic Information on Prescribing by General Practitioners" _BMJ_, September 7 1963, Vol.11, pp 599-604.

Wolman, L. _Ebb and Flow of Trade Unions_, National Bureau of Economic Reserach, New York, 1936.

Wright, D.M. (ed) _The Impact of the Union_, Harcourt Brace & Co. New York, 1951.

Yarrow, G. "Trade Unions and Economic Welfare", _IEA Readings 17_, IEA London, 1978, pp 55-57.

Index

175